THE
BOOK
OF
BOXES

THE
BOOK
OF
BOXES

ANDREW CRAWFORD

RUNNING PRESS
PHILADELPHIA, PENNSYLVANIA

9 8 7 6 5 4 3 2 1
Digit on the right indicates the number of this printing.

ISBN 1-56138-290-6

Library of Congress Cataloging-in-Publication Number 93-83518

This book was designed and produced by

Quarto Inc
The Old Brewery
6 Blundell Street
London N7 9BH

Senior editor Kate Kirby
Editors Mike Collins, Lydia Darbyshire, Bob Flexner
Senior art editor Amanda Bakhtiar
Designer Karin Skanberg
Picture researcher Anna Kobryn
Photographers Martin Norris, Chas Wilder
Illustrations Rob Shone, Elsa Godfrey, David Kemp (plans)
Picture manager Rebecca Horsewood
Art director Moira Clinch
Publishing director Janet Slingsby
Cover designer Toby Schmidt

Publisher's Note:
Woodworking can be dangerous. Both hand and power tools can quickly sever
nerves, tendons or limbs. Always exercise extreme caution. Always read the
instruction manuals and use the safety guards provided.

As far as the methods and techniques mentioned in this book are concerned,
all statements, information and advice given here are believed to be true and
accurate. However, neither the author, copyright holder nor the publisher can
accept any legal liability for errors or omissions.

The boxes shown in the gallery section of this
book are the copyright of the individual box-makers, and may not be
reproduced for commercial purposes.

Typeset by En to En, Tunbridge Wells
Manufactured in Singapore by Bright Arts (Singapore) Pte. Ltd
Printed in Hong Kong by Lee-Fung Asco Printers Ltd

This book may be ordered by mail from the publisher. Please include $2.50 for
postage and handling. *But try your bookstore first!*

Running Press Book Publishers
125 South Twenty-second Street
Philadelphia, Pennsylvania 19103-4399

Walnut, maple, and mahogany are the woods chosen for these elegant, easy-to-make little boxes.

A delightful trunk-style box with solid domed lid, piano hinge, and catch.

A striking playing card box with sliding lid and veneer lining.

An elegant pencil box featuring a tilting lid.

CONTENTS

INTRODUCTION

A BOX IS a closed container, traditionally rectangular and made of wood, in which all manner of items are kept, collected, protected, hoarded, preserved, hidden, displayed, or forgotten. It is no great feat to make a box that works, but care and attention are needed to produce a box that is mechanically sound, is pleasing to the eye, and fulfills its function efficiently.

The Book of Boxes has been written to cater for all levels of ability, from beginner to accomplished woodworker, and for those with only a few hand tools to those with a whole workshop full of advanced woodworking machinery. It shows that with careful planning and a little practice, a wide variety of boxes of all types can be made. The book advises the reader on the tools and equipment that are needed to make the boxes. It then describes, step-by-step, the making from scratch of 10 boxes of different styles, constructions, and levels of difficulty. Some are functional; some are fanciful; but all feature in this practical, informative, and easy-to-use book.

The section on decorative techniques is intended to encourage readers to personalize their chosen project by choosing from a wide variety of techniques, including marquetry, parquetry, and making inlays and bandings. An inspirational gallery of work by some of today's finest makers completes what is the essential book for woodworkers of all standards who want to investigate this fascinating branch of their craft.

HOW TO USE THIS BOOK

The projects in this book are arranged by degree of difficulty, so if you are a novice boxmaker, begin with a project toward the beginning. Different decorative effects are demonstrated in the projects, and later chapters look in more detail at further decorative effects and finishing methods. Each box-making project comes with its own plans and cutting list and a list of tools and materials you will need.

CUTTING LIST
For the most part, the cutting lists are given in finished sizes indicating the dimensions of single components and the number required. This will allow you to see exactly what you need and to decide how best to convert available wood, maybe left over from a larger-scale cabinet-work project.

TOOLKIT
The basic tools for projects are listed on pages 8-13. Tools additional to the basic kit are listed with each project for which they are required.

STEP-BY-STEP ARTWORK
These demonstrate how to make each of the featured boxes. Photographs show the box at key stages in its construction.

** = on the cutting list indicates allowance for cutting off the lid.

* = on the cutting list indicates where extra has been allowed for miters to be cut, or a base to be trimmed square after jointing, and for pieces to be accurately trimmed to size to fit construction steps already carried out.

PLANS
The plans are intended for reference to show clearly the constructional details of each project, but are not given actual size. If desired, the plans can be enlarged by photocopying, but the precise proportions as drawn should not be taken literally.

WOODS TO USE
Alternative woods to those used in the projects. This list is not definitive, and you may wish to experiment with other possibilities.

MATERIALS
What you will need in the way of hardware, or fabric for lining, etc., is listed here.

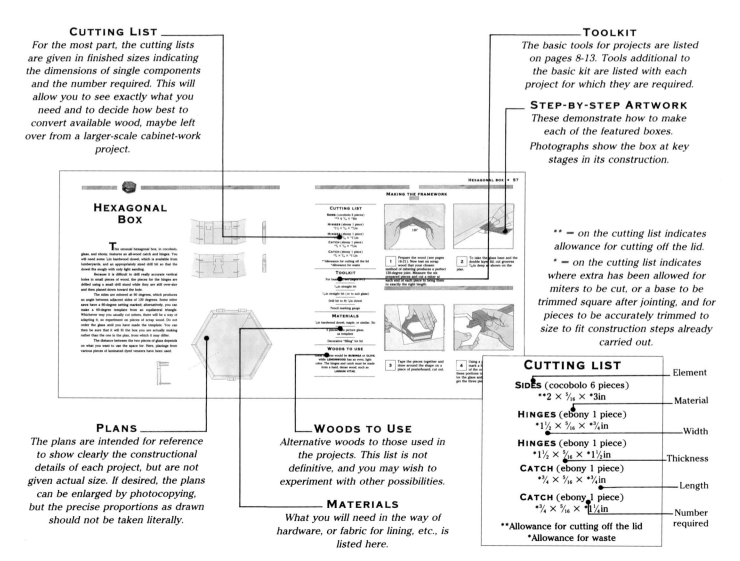

CUTTING LIST

SIDES (cocobolo 6 pieces) — Element / Material
**2 × ⁵/₁₆ × *3in — Width

HINGES (ebony 1 piece)
*1¹/₂ × ⁵/₁₆ × *³/₄in — Thickness

HINGES (ebony 1 piece)
*1¹/₂ × ⁵/₁₆ × *1¹/₂in — Length

CATCH (ebony 1 piece)
*³/₄ × ⁵/₁₆ × *³/₄in

CATCH (ebony 1 piece)
*³/₄ × ⁵/₁₆ × *1¹/₄in — Number required

**Allowance for cutting off the lid
*Allowance for waste

TOOLS AND EQUIPMENT

An anodized-steel, easy-read ruler is best, and a selection of lengths and widths is useful for a variety of measuring and cutting jobs. Those that are regularly used for cutting along should be backed with fine abrasive paper to prevent slipping.

Apart from high-quality measuring and marking instruments, most woodworking tools do not come in a condition in which they can be used immediately. This is especially true of cutting tools, particularly those used in very fine work such as box-making. Most chisels and gouges will need to be ground, honed, buffed, or stropped, while power tools or machines need to be set up, adjusted, and generally fiddled about with.

For this reason, most owners regard their tools as very personal items and are reluctant to lend them to others. Because working practices vary so much from craftsperson to craftsperson, very few woodworkers ever go out and buy tools wholesale. It is far more usual for a collection to be built up slowly, usually by trial and error, with additions usually made simply to suit the latest job in hand. There are, of course, some tools, such as saws, chisels, and marking gauges, that no boxmaker can do without, but even among these, there is much variation in different workshops.

Woodworkers will often improvise and either make or modify a tool to suit a particular need. In box-making, for example, a pencil marking gauge (made simply by substituting a sharp pencil for a steel point in an ordinary marking gauge) can be very useful. In general, always buy the best you can afford. More important, however, is to keep all tools and equipment in tip-top condition; it is simply not possible to produce fine work with inferior or badly conditioned tools.

Shown on the next few pages are the basic items of equipment needed to make the boxes featured in the projects.

TRY-SQUARE

This is an essential tool for the box-maker; it is ideal for marking out and for determining if the edges and sides of wood are square with each other. Some try-squares are fixed, some are adjustable, and some even have a built-in level and calibrated measurements.

Marking gauge used to mark parallel lines.

MARKING GAUGE

Centuries old and fundamentally unchanged since it was first used, the marking gauge is a simple tool with a rod, a fence, and a locking screw or wedge. At the end is a sharp pin, which scribes the mark for the cut. It saves having to measure and re-measure on repetitive cuts.

SCRIBER

A scriber, which can be almost anything with a sharp edge or point, is commonly used to mark very fine dimensions that might be obscured by a pencil point or something of equal thickness. Scribing will also help to prevent "breakout" when coarse-grained woods are cut.

HANDSAW

There are many kinds of handsaw, and they can have anything from 5 to 12 teeth per inch. Their main function is in the conversion of wood from its rough state to sizes ready for planing. A ripsaw is used for cutting along the grain, and a crosscut saw is used for cutting across it. The boxmaker will use handsaws mainly in the initial preparation of the wood.

TENON SAW

More genteel than the handsaw and with up to 16 teeth per inch, the tenon saw can be used for the initial cutting out before a miter box saw or, perhaps, a disk sander is used to achieve the final dimensions. The tenon saw is more likely to find a home in general furniture-making rather than in box-making, but it is a useful addition to the workshop for rapid conversions.

DOVETAIL SAW

The dovetail saw is probably the first of the handsaws to have a real application in finished box-making. It comes with a range of between 18 and 22 teeth per inch, and, as its name implies, it is used primarily for cutting dovetail joints. It is sometimes supplied with a small, round handle, when it is then known as a "gentleman's" saw.

JEWELER'S PIERCING SAW

Particularly useful for very fine work, this little sister of the fretsaw is commonly used in the jewelry trade. In box-making it is used for cutting off the heads of pins and for cutting mother-of-pearl for decorative inlays. It is particularly useful because it has an adjustment that allows it to use broken blades.

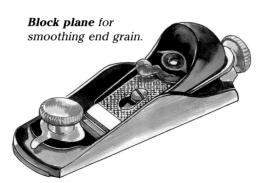

Block plane for smoothing end grain.

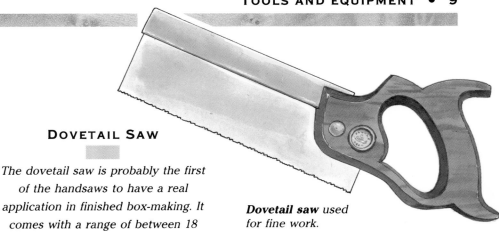

Dovetail saw used for fine work.

BLOCK PLANE

The block plane comes into its own when you have to cut end grain on wood. It achieves this by having a cutting iron that is set at a lower angle than that of the bench planes. This makes it necessary for the bevel to face up in the body rather than down. Unlike most planes, it is used in one hand only. Most block planes have only limited adjustment.

SMOOTHING PLANE

For most box-making and other small-scale woodworking, the largest plane you are likely to need is a cabinetmaker's smoothing plane – this takes the place of a "jack" plane, which is normally used to remove the saw marks from rough-sawn wood for larger-scale cabinet-work. Set fine, this useful multi-purpose plane will perform most of the operations needed for box-making.

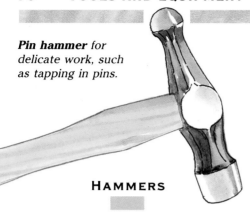

Pin hammer for delicate work, such as tapping in pins.

HAMMERS

Although they are not the most sophisticated of tools, hammers are nonetheless essential. Tapping in pins in miter work or other delicate joint making will require a small, delicate tool, but it is handy to have one or two heavier hammers in the workshop for general use.

CHISELS

There is a bewildering variety of chisels from which to choose – they are the bread-and-butter tools of hand work. They are used for fine paring, cutting-in locks and hinges, cutting end grain, among a dozen and one other applications.

MALLET

The mallet is used primarily for driving chisels and gouges when a steel hammer would damage a wooden handle. When you are carving, a mallet is easier to control because it is larger and heavier than a hammer.

SCREWDRIVERS

Most workshops contain a good selection, but in box-making only a few of the smaller sizes are really necessary, and these are usually needed for installing hinges.

BAR CLAMPS

Another fundamental piece of workshop equipment, these come in an array of shapes and sizes. They can be all metal, all wood, or wood and metal. Most work well, but always remember not to overtighten them; this can cause bruising if the wood is not protected, but more often will cause the parts being glued to slip or even break.

C CLAMPS

These are available in a range of throat depths so that pressure can be applied in a variety of places. They are capable of exerting a great deal of pressure in one spot, and they should, therefore, always be used with scrap-wood spacers to prevent bruising. Cheap ones often break or bend in use, although in box-making it is unlikely that enough pressure would be used for this to happen.

CRAFT KNIFE

Surgical precision can be obtained through the use of a craft knife, which makes it an invaluable tool in box-making. It can be used for a thousand and one jobs, including simple marking, template-making, and inlaying. Craft knives generally come with a variety of disposable blades, which are individually wrapped and razor sharp.

CABINET SCRAPER

A cabinet scraper is by far the best-value tool you will ever buy. It is simply a rectangle of steel, available in a variety of sizes and thicknesses which, when correctly sharpened, is the ultimate smoothing tool, used by cabinetmakers for centuries. Choose a fairly small, flexible scraper for small work such as box-making.

SHARPENING STONES

You will need fine stones for delicate work, and most people use diamond-impregnated stones. There are many systems that can be used for sharpening, and it is a subject worth a great deal of exploration. Generally speaking, a boxmaker will need to find either a very fine finishing stone or a system that uses abrasive pastes on a buffing wheel.

THICKNESSING GAUGE

This tool, which is similar to a micrometer, has a deep throat that can gauge the thickness of wood extremely accurately. Beloved by the makers of musical instruments, it has found its way into box-making by virtue of its accuracy and because it can provide a "read out" on a dial at all points.

ELECTRIC DRILL

Cheap, handy, and versatile, the electric drill has probably done more to revolutionize the woodworking trade than any other single development in the last 50 years. A stand-mounted electric drill is most relevant to box-making.

DRILL BIT SELECTION

Other than suggesting that any collection should begin with the finest and work up, it is impossible to say what the boxmaker will use when it comes to drill bits. "Lip and spur" drills are best for drilling clean, accurately placed holes, but are not available in the smallest sizes. Your own preferences and working methods will dictate your choice, and as you decide your areas of interest, so your collection will grow.

Portable electric drill, handy to have in the workshop.

DRILL STAND

This is an indispensable item when holes need to be drilled absolutely vertically, as when making wooden hinges. It is also useful to have the drill mounted static for drilling holes in fine hinge stock held supported by a piece of scrap. With the use of a small, improvised "table" and a small sanding drum, it can also be used to sand curved components.

BANDSAW

The bandsaw is almost certainly the safest power tool in the workshop, and it has also proved itself to be one of the most versatile. It is particularly useful for cutting curves. It can accommodate a variety of blades, it runs quietly and smoothly, and it seldom damages fingers. It is especially useful for template cutting, which is of great value to boxmakers.

PLANER-THICKNESSER

Although you can survive without one, a planer-thicknesser will make you happy. It is not a necessary tool, but it will eliminate hours of hand planing and usually, if properly set up, will produce correctly dimensioned wood ready to be worked on.

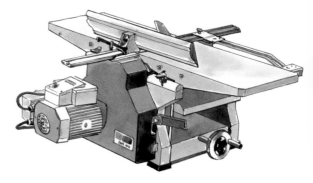

Planer-thicknesser primarily used for thicknessing.

DISK SANDER

The disk sander is capable of extremely fine work. Usually fitted with a fence to travel through 45 to 90 degrees and capable of being fitted with sandpapers of all grits, it really comes into its own when taken to really fine dimensions. Boxmakers find it invaluable when taking off dimensions that have no sensible equivalents on rulers.

ROUTER

A king among tools, the router is almost indispensable in box-making. It can be used freehand, locked overhead, inverted on a table, or simply run against fences. It will cut templates, shapes, and profiles and, with a selection of bits, almost any molding you want. Used normally – and with carbide bits – it will stay sharp about 50 times longer than a molding plane.

SELECTION OF ROUTER BITS

As with drill bits, the selection of router bits must be a personal one. Carbide bits offer better value for money, but they are much more expensive. Bits with a bottom-cutting facility are certainly more useful for box-making, because depths when cutting out for a stringing are crucial.

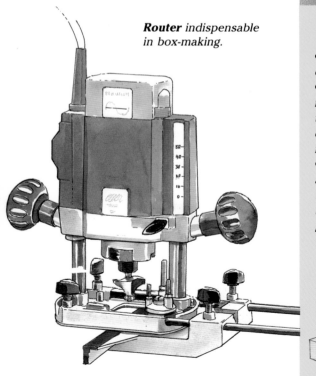

Router *indispensable in box-making.*

ROUTING TIPS

- *A fine screw height adjuster is essential for fine work.*
- *When you buy straight cutters, remember that two flutes are better than one and make sure that the cutters have a "bottom cut" for routing grooves and rebates.*
- *When cutting along end grain, always back the work onto the cutter to halve its diameter before you begin, to avoid splitting away the grain at the end of the full cut.*

- *For decorative cuts in end grain, start the cut slightly shallower than required and finish with a fine, full-depth cut. This avoids scorching the wood. Using a slower than usual speed also helps.*
- *For many of the routing operations in this book, a right-angle guide is essential. Actual dimensions are unimportant, but the pieces must meet at exactly 90 degrees (see diagram, below).*

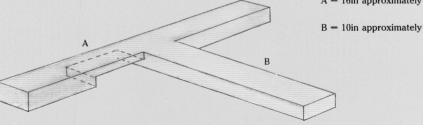

A = 16in approximately

B = 10in approximately

TOOL MAINTENANCE

- *A good woodworker does not regard tool maintenance as a chore – it is simply second nature. However, no one wants to be sharpening tools for hours when other jobs are pressing, so the ideal is to avoid maintenance if at all possible. Among the most obvious ways of achieving this are always keeping tools in clean, dry conditions to prevent rust and corrosion, and always replacing the tip guards of cutting tools such as saws and chisels after using them. Chisels are best kept in racks rather than in*

drawers so that cutting edges do not touch metal. Planes should be laid on their sides on the bench when they are not in use, and when you have finished with them completely, the blade should be withdrawn just inside the sole for complete protection.

There will, inevitably, come a time when chisels need to be sharpened. A few rubs on a good stone followed by buffing or stropping should be adequate, but if they need to be re-ground, use a large diameter, slow-turning, wet wheel and grind them to

approximately 25 degrees. Follow this by honing on a stone to a second bevel of 30 degrees.

Most power tools require very little maintenance other than blade adjustments, replacement belts and so forth.

Demonstrated on this page is the correct way to sharpen a cabinet scraper. If blunt, this important tool is worse than useless; a keen scraper on the other hand, can take off the finest of shavings to produce a smooth surface not always possible with a plane.

SHARPENING A SCRAPER

1 Both edges need to be straight and square. Do this by working the scraper first upright, then flat on a good, flat, fine oilstone. This should produce the profile shown.

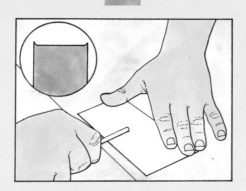

2 Hold the scraper flat on a work surface so that one edge is about ½in in from the edge. Firmly rub along this edge with the back of a carving gouge or scraper burnisher, with the handle tilted down slightly to draw over a fine "hook" as shown. Repeat for the other edges.

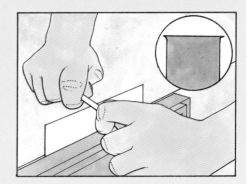

3 Work the gouge or burnisher along the scraper's upturned edge. Exert firm pressure, tilting it slightly one way, then the other, to turn the "hook" over and produce the profile shown. Repeat to make four good, sharp edges.

CHOOSING WOOD

Some extremely exotic and rare woods are used in box-making. This is because the quantities required are normally small, and the boxes are often made to store highly personal, valuable or sentimental items. The availability of such wood varies enormously from country to country and even from place to place, so that the choice of wood may, in fact, be limited to what is available.

Problems associated with cabinet-making, such as warping, checks, and twistings, are less likely to affect the box-maker because mainly short lengths are used, and the longer and wider lengths will be quarter-sawn. It is worth searching lumberyards for cutoffs and small leftover pieces. When you buy from a lumberyard, always go in person if possible. You are the only person who knows exactly what you want, and you may see something you had not previously considered which may be as good as, or better than, your first choice.

Selecting wood that is free from knots, checks, and warping and that has the required rays or figuring will be a matter of eye if you are on the spot and the wood is converted, or a question of pot luck if you are not or it isn't. You may find you have to buy more than you need to get the piece you want.

You will, however, probably buy most of your wood by mail or by phone, and you will be at the mercy of the salesman. Most wood suppliers are easy to deal with and will be prepared for you to return goods if you're not satisfied. There is no quality control to dictate that one piece of walnut is the same as another or that maple will always behave in the same way.

AMERICAN YELLOW PINE

Straight-grained and evenly textured, this wood will take very fine detailing. It is, therefore, ideal for a box with carved features of any sort. The wood works easily, screws and glues well, and is also extremely stable. Its unremarkable appearance can easily be enhanced by the use of inlays and bandings. In addition to its excellent working properties, it can be brought to a very fine finish.

AMERICAN WALNUT

Dark and sensuous, this wood is ideal for working in the solid, for it could be described as "craftsperson friendly" in every respect. It has no major drawbacks: it will screw, glue, nail, and shine as required. It will take stain and French-polish easily, it will work well, and it has only a moderate blunting effect on tools.

AUSTRALIAN BLACKWOOD

Rich and lustrous, with a distinctly dark brown rather than black appearance, this wood is ideal for a box for a special occasion or to hold real treasures. It stains and French-polishes very pleasingly, but it can be sometimes difficult to screw or nail.

CHERRY

A fine, even texture coupled with some delicate flecking make this a very attractive wood. A straight grain makes it pleasing to work for the boxmaker, as does its willingness to glue easily and hold screws and nails well. It is not totally problem-free, however: it will tear in the cross-grain, which can make planing a problem, and it will warp easily, although with the sizes used in box-making this is unlikely to be a problem. It redeems itself by taking a fine finish with no fuss.

EBONY

Often jet black or strikingly figured with brown stripes, ebony is hard, stable, dense, and brittle when used against both hand and powered cutting tools. In box-making it scores highly in the making of stringings, bandings, and moldings. It requires pre-boring for screwing or nailing, and care is required when glue is used. On the plus side, though, are the facts that it will French-polish to a magnificent finish and it is extremely durable.

EUROPEAN PLANE

Quartered boards produce a fine, flecked figure known as lacewood, and this attractive, subtle wood is ideal for the boxmaker. The fine medium texture works well, but you will need sharp tools.

HOLLY

Holly is plain white with a fine, even texture – some woodworkers regard it as a rather bland wood. It is often used as a substitute for boxwood, or, dyed, as a substitute for ebony. In box-making it can be used solid for smaller items, but it is also available as a veneer. You will need sharp tools because it is difficult to cut.

INDIAN ROSEWOOD

Fragrant and warming, this striking timber is highly valued and difficult to work, and is often found only in veneers. It severely blunts cutting tools and often contains calcareous deposits, which can wreak havoc with them. It can be used in box-making either solid or as veneer, and it more than makes up for its shortcomings by being amenable to polished or waxed finishes in a way that few other woods can match.

KINGWOOD

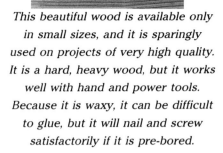

This beautiful wood is available only in small sizes, and it is sparingly used on projects of very high quality. It is a hard, heavy wood, but it works well with hand and power tools. Because it is waxy, it can be difficult to glue, but it will nail and screw satisfactorily if it is pre-bored.

ROCK MAPLE

Although it can sometimes be bland in appearance, some logs will produce a bird's-eye figure that is prized for its decorative veneers. In the solid, the irregular grain will sometimes be a problem, and sharp tools are essential. The heavy wood is ideal for smaller boxes, making them pleasantly tactile. It is difficult to nail without pre-boring, but will glue very easily.

YEW

Yew is not easy to work as it will tear on the cross-grain, but it will bend like rubber when steamed. Its high oil content can make gluing a problem, and screwing and nailing are not easy. The color of the stripes can vary from cream to purple. It will also stain well – but who would want to do that?

PLANNING AND PREPARATION

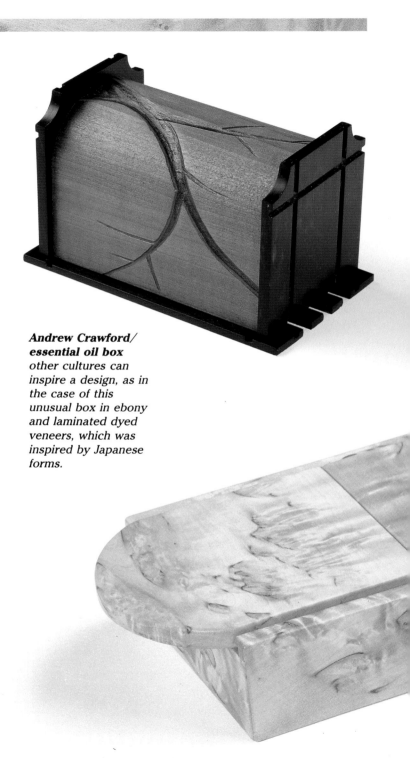

All the boxes included in *The Book of Boxes* are basically nothing more than wood wrapped around space in various ways, either for a particular purpose or for no purpose at all.

If you are relatively new to woodworking, it is probably better if you follow the designs as they are laid out and described in the following projects. As you develop a feel for the design and construction of boxes, however, or if you are already an experienced woodworker, you may feel confident to adapt these designs to create your own boxes, either influenced by the fine work in the gallery section or working entirely from your own imagination. However you approach it, though, your box will need to be planned.

Andrew Crawford/ ***essential oil box*** *other cultures can inspire a design, as in the case of this unusual box in ebony and laminated dyed veneers, which was inspired by Japanese forms.*

BALANCE AND PROPORTION

When you are planning a box, several criteria need to be considered, and they are not necessarily the same as those that are relevant to cabinet work. Boxes designed and built by professional cabinet makers often, although by no means always, tend to be on the chunky side because they are made from material that is rather too thick for the dimensions of the piece. When you select your materials, err on the side of using thinner, rather than thicker, wood, and you will produce well-proportioned, balanced pieces. On the other hand, of course, if you want to exaggerate the solidity and weight of a box, that is a specific requirement that must be considered at the design stage.

John Anderson/
peacock box *about as impractical as a box can get – but a functional box nevertheless, planned with stunning visual effect as the main criterion.*

David Gregson/
sliding-lid box *the elegantly shaped and overlong two-part sliding lid is an interesting feature on this otherwise simple box in mazur birch.*

TECHNIQUES

A box can be made as a pure, free expression, as a flight of fancy with no underlying purpose, in which case you are not bound by any functional or practical restraints. Most people, however, find that it is easier to design a box when they have a particular function in mind – a container for pencils, jewelry, or playing cards, for example. If you have a specific purpose in mind for your box, you must make clear, accurate drawings, preferably working from the inside out. First, draw exactly to scale the space you need to create *inside* the box. Then draw the box around the *outside*. You do not have to be a draftsman, but you will find that a full-size, perspective drawing, however rough, will help you to visualize and design the external and decorative aspects of the box.

Experienced cabinet makers may have some doubts about one or two of the constructional techniques used here – unstrengthened, glued miters, for example. However, it is important to remember that you are working to a much smaller scale, and the stresses applied to a box are a lot less than those that a table, chair, or chest is designed to withstand. A miter is an excellent joint to use for box-making and many other, small-scale woodworking projects. A well-cut miter generates a relatively large area for gluing and any constructional details – grooves for the base, rabbets for the lid, decorative beading, and so on – are automatically transferred around the whole framework, inside and out, without having to work corners separately by hand, as has to be done with rabbeted or dovetailed corners. If necessary, miters can be easily strengthened by horizontal splines, both internal (hidden) or external (decorative), or by vertical tongues. In any case, experienced woodworkers will probably be adapting these designs and can change any constructional details.

If you are making a small box with a solid lid for which you are using wood up to, say, 3 inches wide, the way in which the wood has been cut and the exact method of construction are not critical. If, however, you wish to enlarge any of the designs given here, it is advisable to use veneered birch plywood for the lid or base instead of solid wood. If you still wish to use solid wood, you must take into consideration the cross-grain expansion and contraction of the wood resulting from seasonal humidity and temperature changes and the gradual, unavoidable shrinkage caused by moisture loss over a long period of time.

The larger the panel, the more important it is that it is made from quarter-sawn wood. This is more stable, less prone to warps and twists and will tend to shrink only about one-third to one-half as much as plane-sawn wood. A frame-and-panel construction of some sort must be used, and the panel must fit snugly all around the edge. Only a minimum amount of glue should be used so that the panel can shrink over time without splitting.

You must, of course, design your box with your available facilities in mind. Most keen woodworkers will own a router, which when mounted under a bought or improvised table is an invaluable tool for all fine woodworking applications of this sort. If you do not own one, now may well be the time to get one.

If, however, you do not own a router, but you do have a collection of old but good rabbet, shoulder, plow, and molding planes or a good-quality combination plane in working order, you will, with practice, be able to do most of the routing operations in this book with these.

Even if you are dedicated to your router, one concession to old-style tools you might like to make is to buy

John Ambrose/ turned box turned boxes need planning, too. Like any other, this piece probably started life as several rough sketches followed by a final, accurate plan.

one or two "hollow" planes. These are invaluable for producing concave sections, which are difficult and time-consuming to make in any other way without specialist tooling. The jewelry box in burl veneer on pages 82-93 is an example of this.

PREPARING WOOD

Whether you have chosen to follow exactly one of the designs included in this book, whether you have adapted one of the designs, or whether you have designed your own box from scratch, you must prepare the wood – that is, the lumber must be brought to the right dimensions before you begin the actual construction of the box.

This is a crucial part of the procedure, and you must take care to convert your wood to consistent dimensions and to make sure that every face is perfectly square and flat. If you have a planer-thicknesser, this job is made far easier and quicker, but remember that you should always allow a little extra length because the knives will tend to dig in at the beginning and end of each pass, leaving 1-2 inches of slightly thinner stock there.

Finally, always allow longer to make a box than you think it will take. This is true of most woodworking projects, but even more so with boxes, especially complex ones. Remember, the art of box-making involves an awful lot of effort being concentrated into a small space.

Overleaf are shown the 12 wood preparation steps to follow before embarking on the projects demonstrated in this book.

PLANING HINTS

- *In order to keep the sole level, downward pressure should always be exerted at the front of the plane at the beginning of a pass (1), evenly distributed when the complete sole is on the work, (2) and transferred to the back as the front of the sole leaves the work (3).*

1 Downward pressure at front of plane

2 Evenly distributed pressure

3 Downward pressure on back of plane

- *Always plane end grain in incomplete passes, working inward from the edges. This helps to prevent the wood at the edges from splitting when the plane leaves the work.*
- *Always keep the iron sharp and set fine for small work.*
- *It is worth knowing how much wood your plane removes with each pass. See how many passes it takes to remove, say, $\frac{1}{32}$in: three to four is about right for converting rough-sawn timber; five to seven are suitable for most fine planing; and eight to nine passes are probably required for end grain work. If it takes more than 10, you could be planing all day.*
- *When you use the step-and-stop set up to plane edges and end grain, pressure should be exerted diagonally downward, toward the edge of the wood with the side of the plane against the bench.*

Pressure exerted diagonally

ROUGH SAWING

1 Set up the bandsaw with a high fence. You may need to build one, and this will be worthwhile because it will mean that you produce pieces of a consistent thickness, particularly when you are using wide, thin stock that you need to make thinner.

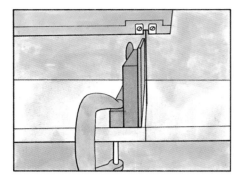

2 All bandsaw blades have a "set" – that is, the teeth are offset to left and right. Measuring from a left-hand set tooth at top and bottom, place the fence measurement at $\frac{1}{16}$–$\frac{3}{32}$in more than your required thickness to allow for planing off the bandsaw marks.

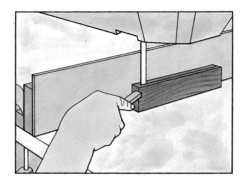

3 The bandsaw is now ready to use. Set the fence carefully and hold the wood firmly and squarely against this, not the table. Switch on and feed the wood through, using a safety push-stick as you near the end of your cut.

PLANING TO THICKNESS

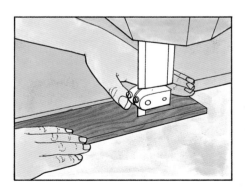

4 Now the wood needs to be cut to width. Place the fence (it can be an ordinary, low one) to $\frac{1}{16}$–$\frac{3}{32}$in more than the required width to allow for the set of the teeth. Feed in any wood you need to convert to this width.

5 If you have a planer-thicknesser, planing to the required thickness is straightforward, but remember to make the pieces a little longer because the knives will tend to dig in at the end of the cut. A powered hand plane can also be used – with care.

6 If you are planing by hand, you will need to set up a stop to hold the pieces while you work them. A single piece, slightly thinner than the piece you are working, is all that is needed. Start to remove the saw marks with a smoothing plane.

PLANING TO SIZE

7 Once you have removed all the saw marks, the piece should be near your required thickness. The final work should be done with a small block plane or a smoothing plane. Work slowly and carefully, removing only fine shavings until you reach the correct thickness.

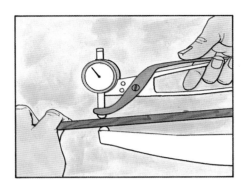

8 The thickness can be measured at the edges using a small steel ruler, but the most accurate method is to use a thicknessing gauge, a tool designed to measure the thickness of guitar soundboards over their whole area.

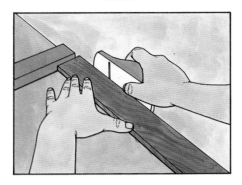

9 Now plane the timber exactly to width. For this you will need a step-and-stop set-up (see opposite, step 6). First, remove all saw marks from one edge. Then work on the other edge and continue until you reach exactly the right thickness.

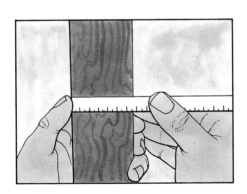

10 Measuring the width is best done using a steel ruler. Hold your left thumb to the left-hand edge of the piece and hold the rule against it. Read the measurement at the right-hand edge. Measure at least both ends and the middle.

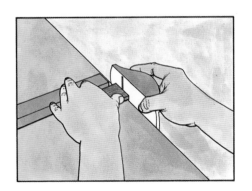

11 Using the same step-and-stop set-up and with one long edge against the stop, plane one end square. Remember to work inward from each edge to avoid breaking away the corners. For very narrow sections, set up the disk sander with a 90-degree fence.

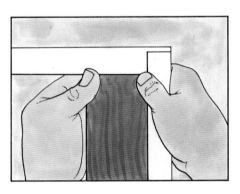

12 Check for perfect squareness. Now measure and mark the required length with a scriber. Bandsaw fractionally over-length and plane this end square and exactly to length. Repeat these steps for each piece required for your chosen project.

Box-making Projects

As you work through these projects, taking them step by step, you will grow in skill and confidence. Begin with the very simplest before undertaking the intermediate range of specialist boxes for pencils and playing cards and the fine jewelry container made in burl veneers.

THREE BASIC BOXES

TOOLKIT

For basic kit, see pages 8-13

Right-angle miter-gauge guide

$\frac{1}{8}$in radius pin or ball-bearing guided corner-round bit

$\frac{1}{4}$in diameter radius bit

Miter saw or disk sander

WOODS TO USE

Almost any fine-grained hardwood is suitable for use on these simple projects and the ones chosen here, **MAHOGANY**, **MAPLE**, and **WALNUT**, serve the purpose well. They can be easily interchanged from project to project, or you might like to use **CHERRY**, **YEW**, or **EBONY** for a really rich finish.

Walnut, mahogany, and maple have been used for these elegant, easy-to-make boxes, but you can, of course, choose your own favorite woods. None of these projects requires any hardware – the lids are all loose and are designed to drop or slide neatly into place.

The completed boxes can either be finished as they are or further decorated using some of the ideas you will find later in the book (see pages 94-113).

Three basic boxes for keepsakes and knickknacks. These boxes have been sealed and waxed, but more elaborate decorative effects could be applied.

BOX IN WALNUT

CUTTING LIST

FRONT/BACK (walnut 2 pieces)
$1\frac{1}{2} \times \frac{1}{4} \times 4\frac{3}{4}$in

SIDES (walnut 2 pieces)
$1\frac{1}{2} \times \frac{1}{4} \times 2\frac{3}{8}$in

LID

(walnut 1 piece)
*$2\frac{3}{4} \times \frac{11}{32} \times$ *5in

BASE

(walnut 1 piece)
*$2\frac{3}{8} \times \frac{1}{8} \times$ *$4\frac{9}{16}$in

*Allowance for waste

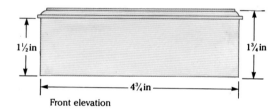

Front elevation

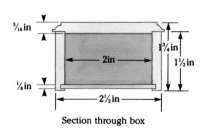

Section through box

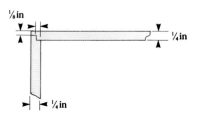

Detail of joint plan

CUTTING THE JOINTS

First prepare the wood (see pages 16-21). Then prepare the joints. At this stage a router and table should be used. This is by far the easiest and most accurate way of forming this joint, but if you do not have one, cut the joint as shown in step 3, below.

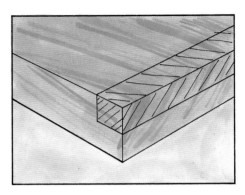

| **1** | To make the rabbets using a router you will need a straight bit at least $\frac{3}{8}$in in diameter. |

Set the fence so that the lateral cut is $\frac{1}{8}$in and set the height to $\frac{1}{8}$in plus. Test the dimensions of the cut on scrap wood first.

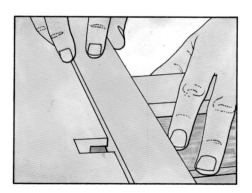

| **2** | Holding the first piece firmly in a right-angle miter gauge, cut a rabbet at each end. Repeat |

with the other three pieces.

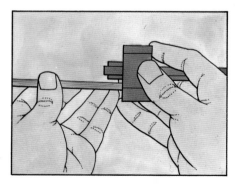

| **3** | If you do not have a router, set a marking gauge to exactly half the thickness of the sides |

and scribe along the ends of each piece on the inside face, across top and bottom edges, and along the end grain. Crosshatch this area for clarity.

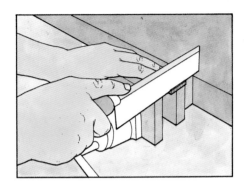

| | Remove this piece by sawing down just outside the line using a fine dovetail saw. Remove the waste with a sharp 1-1½in wide chisel. Trim back to the scribed lines, leaving the tongues fractionally over-length. Repeat this for both ends of each piece. |
|**4**| |

| | Lay out the pieces as shown above and number each joint separately. Trim the tongue of each end by planing until each joint is a snug fit. |
|**5**| |

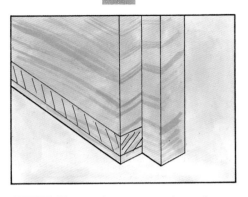

| | Now make a groove in each side to take the base. Set up the router with a ⅛in straight bit to cut a groove ⅛in deep and ³⁄₆₄in from the bottom of the sides. |
|**6**| |

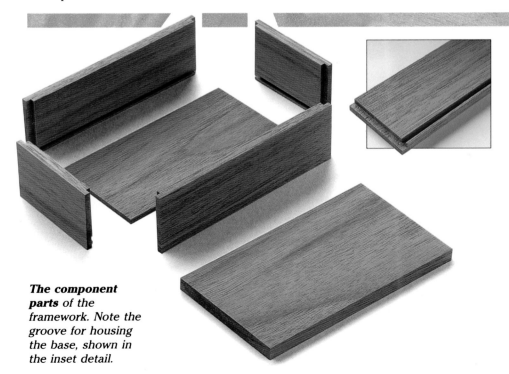

The component parts of the framework. Note the groove for housing the base, shown in the inset detail.

| | Sand the base and the four prepared sides. If the joints are well cut, small bodies like this can be taped together for gluing. Assemble as shown without glue and check for fit and squareness. If you are satisfied, take apart and repeat with glue. |
|**7**| |

FITTING THE LID

BOX IN MAHOGANY

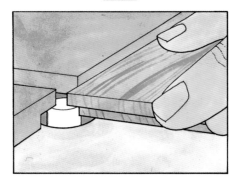

8 Now cut the shallow rabbet around the underneath of the lid – this locates the lid on the framework. Using a ³⁄₈in or larger bit, set the router to cut a depth of ¹⁄₁₆in and start to cut to a conservative width, widening the cut until the lid falls into place.

9 Finally, using a corner-round bit with a pin or ball-bearing guide, cut the decoration around the lid. Sand the box smooth. It is now ready for further decoration and finishing (see pages 94-123).

CUTTING LIST

FRONT/BACK (mahogany 2 pieces)
1³⁄₄ × ¹⁄₄ × *5in

SIDES (mahogany 2 pieces)
1³⁄₄ × ¹⁄₄ × *2³⁄₄in

LID

PANEL (mahogany 1 piece)
*2¹⁄₂ × ¹⁄₄ × *4³⁄₄in

BASE
(mahogany 1 piece)
3¹⁄₄ × ⁹⁄₃₂ × *5¹⁄₂in

*Allowance for waste

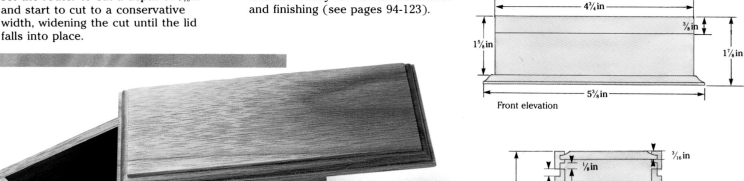

Front elevation

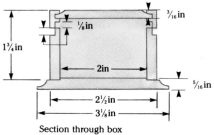

Section through box

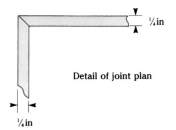

Detail of joint plan

The finished box
showing the corner-round decoration on the lid.

CUTTING THE JOINTS

LID AND FRAMEWORK

First prepare the wood (see pages 16-21). Mark the exact lengths required on the pieces for the sides with a scriber – these define the outside of the pieces. Cut just outside these lines on the bandsaw, using the 45-degree guide, or on a miter saw.

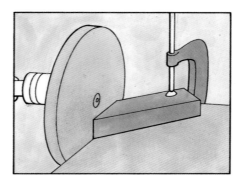

1 Trim exactly to length using the disk sander and accurate 45-degree fence. Making your own fence for temporary use is a simple task.

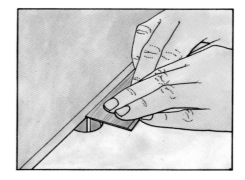

2 Make two grooves on the inside of each side using a $\frac{1}{8}$in straight bit, in the positions shown in the plans. These grooves are to take the lid and form one half of the lid-locating lip respectively.

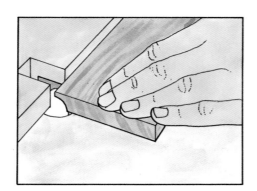

3 The lid must now be shaped to fit into the upper of the two grooves. Use a $\frac{9}{16}$in-diameter radius bit adjusted to leave $\frac{1}{8}$in thickness at the lid's edge. The lid should, in any case, fit snugly into its groove. Repeat for the base while the router is set up.

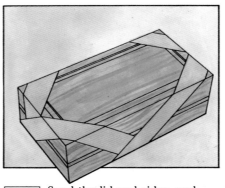

4 Sand the lid and sides, and tape them together to check for general fit and squareness, also sanding the lid edges if necessary.

A close-up of the miter and grooves at the end of one of the sides. The lid fits into the top groove, and the bottom groove forms one half of the lid-locating lip.

The parts of the box
ready for assembly.

| 5 | Now apply glue to the miters and a little to the lid groove, and assemble. When the glue is dry, remove the tape and sand the bottom of the sides evenly. |

CUTTING OFF THE LID

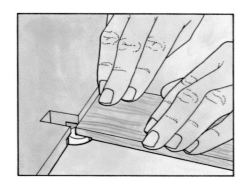

| 6 | Cut the shallow rabbet around the base to locate it into the bottom of the box. Work slowly, increasing the width of the cut gradually until the base just slots into place. |

| 7 | Measure from the base to the bottom of the lip groove. Set up the table with a $\frac{1}{8}$in straight bit, and set a distance from the fence to the edge of the bit to your measurement less $\frac{1}{64}$in. Test on scrap wood first. Depth of cut should be just over $\frac{1}{8}$in. |

| 8 | Cut the groove all the way around the box, with the base against the fence, gradually turning the box onto all four of the sides. |

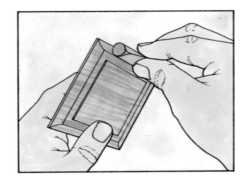

9 Carefully part the lid from the rest of the box with a craft knife and clean the rough edges. The lid should fit snugly over its lip – if you're lucky it may fit all the way around!

10 Sand the base, glue it in place, and clamp gently. When it is dry, sand the whole box with fine sandpaper. It is now ready for additional decoration and finishing (see pages 94-123).

The complete box *ready for the decorative finish of your choice.*

BOX IN MAPLE

CUTTING LIST

FRONT/BACK (maple 2 pieces)
$1\frac{1}{2} \times \frac{1}{4} \times$ *5in

SIDES (maple 2 pieces)
$1\frac{1}{2} \times \frac{1}{4} \times$ *2$\frac{3}{4}$in

LID
(maple 1 piece)
*$2\frac{1}{2} \times \frac{1}{4} \times$ *4$\frac{3}{4}$in

BASE
(maple 1 piece)
*$2\frac{1}{2} \times \frac{5}{32} \times 4 \times$ *4$\frac{3}{4}$in

*Allowance for waste

MAKING THE FRAMEWORK

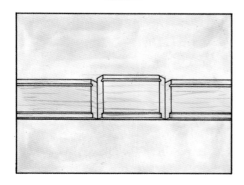

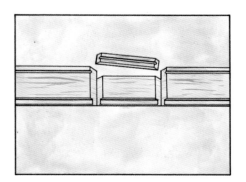

1 Having prepared the wood (see pages 16-21), miter the four pieces for the sides. Make a $\frac{1}{8}$in groove for the lid on the inside of each side, $\frac{1}{8}$in deep, and a rabbet for the base $\frac{3}{16}$in wide and $\frac{3}{16}$in deep.

2 Saw the wide end in two longitudinally, leaving $\frac{1}{8}$in below the groove. Plane the bottom half so that its top edge is $\frac{3}{32}$in below the bottom of the grooves of its adjacent sides.

Front view of finished box showing lid slightly out

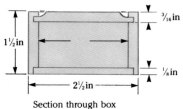

$1\frac{1}{2}$in

$4\frac{3}{4}$in

Shows portion of end that is attached to end of lid

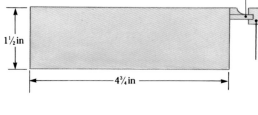

$\frac{3}{16}$in

$1\frac{1}{2}$in

$\frac{1}{8}$in

$2\frac{1}{2}$in

Section through box

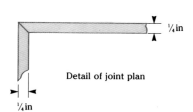

$\frac{1}{4}$in

Detail of joint plan

$\frac{1}{4}$in

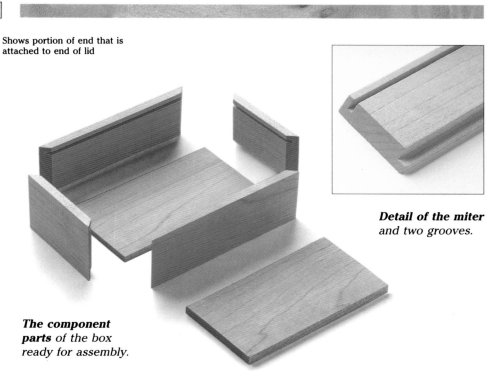

The component parts of the box ready for assembly.

Detail of the miter and two grooves.

THREE BASIC BOXES • 31

FITTING LID AND BASE

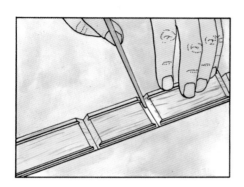

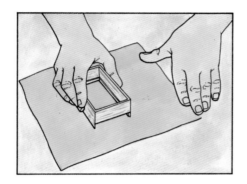

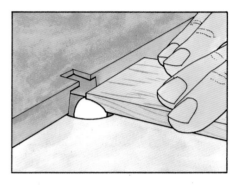

3 Sand the sides and tape them together to check for general fit and squareness. Apply glue to the miters and reassemble.

4 When it is dry, remove the tape and sand the top and bottom of the sides even with a gentle movement over sandpaper on a flat surface.

5 Shape the lid edges using a $9/16$in-diameter radius bit. Glue the top half of the wide side to the end of the lid centrally. When dry, plane the underneath side until the lid slips into place.

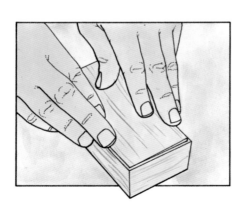

6 Plane the base to size, sand and glue in place with light clamping if necessary. Sand the whole box with fine sandpaper. It is now ready for further decorating and finishing.

The sliding lid box
ready for finishing.

TRUNK-STYLE BOX

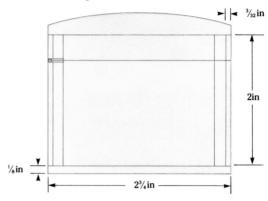

Section through box

$^3/_{32}$ in

2 in

$^1/_8$ in

2$^3/_4$ in

This traditional trunk-style box is made in walnut. It was built using one of the simplest of all box-making techniques: the sides are joined using a single rabbet joint, the lid and base are glued onto the framework, and the lid is cut off on a router table after the whole piece has been assembled and glued.

The glued-on base and lid give an attractive, darker end grain, which has the effect of framing the piece and adds to its visual appeal. The inlaid kingwood bandings, which imitate luggage straps, further enhance the appearance.

The catch used here is a miniature version of those used on full-sized trunks and is available from craft and hobby shops. However, any other small catch can be used, and your own choice from the many available will help to personalize the project.

The hinge is a $^1/_2$ in piano hinge, which can be bought from any good hardware store. You simply cut this to length and drill additional holes if necessary.

Front elevation

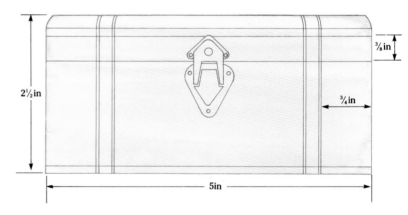

$^3/_8$ in

2$^1/_2$ in

$^3/_4$ in

5 in

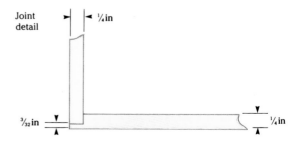

Joint detail

$^1/_4$ in

$^3/_{32}$ in

$^1/_4$ in

MAKING THE FRAMEWORK

CUTTING LIST

FRONT/BACK (walnut 2 pieces)
**$2\frac{1}{8} \times \frac{1}{4} \times 5$in

SIDES (walnut 2 pieces)
**$2\frac{1}{8} \times \frac{1}{4} \times 2\frac{5}{8}$in

LID (walnut 1 piece)
*$3 \times \frac{3}{8} \times *5\frac{3}{32}$in

BASE (walnut 1 piece)
*$3 \times \frac{1}{8} \times *5\frac{3}{32}$in

**Allowance for cutting off the lid
*Allowance for waste

TOOLKIT

For basic kit, see pages 8-13

MATERIALS

6in of $\frac{1}{2}$in piano hinge

A miniature trunk catch or similar locking device

Bandings of your choice

WOODS TO USE

WALNUT was chosen here for its lustrous beauty, which contrasts so well with the inlaid bandings. You may feel that **MAHOGANY** or **BUBINGA** might be more attractive, or it may be that a delicate, pale wood such as **SYCAMORE** could be more what you are looking for.

First prepare the wood (see pages 16-21). A router and router table should be used for this, but if you don't own a router, which is by far the easiest and most efficient way of cutting this joint, see steps 3 and 4 below.

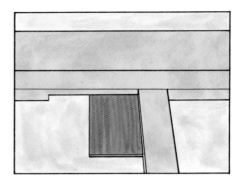

1 To cut the rabbets at the ends of the front and back of the box on the router, you need a straight bit at least $\frac{3}{8}$in in diameter. Set the fence to a height two-thirds the thickness of the ends, to remove exactly the thickness of the ends from the front and back.

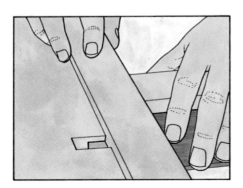

2 Holding the first piece in the right-angle miter gauge, cut a rabbet. Repeat the process at the other end and again at both ends of the other piece to form the matching end.

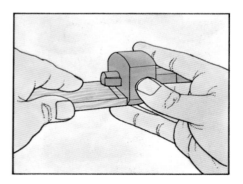

3 These joints can be cut by hand. Set the marking gauge to $\frac{1}{4}$in and mark out as in the plan. Now set to $\frac{11}{64}$in and scribe a line along the end grain of the front and back with the larger part inside. Now scribe a line along the top and bottom to meet the lines there.

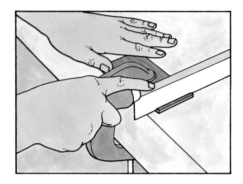

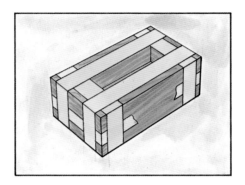

4 Remove these pieces by sawing down just on the waste side of the line using a dovetail saw. Cut away this waste portion with a sharp, wide chisel. Trim back to the scribed lines.

5 Make a template for the lid shape as shown and transfer this shape to both ends of the piece for the lid, planing down to these lines to produce the gentle curve.

6 Sand the four prepared sides and assemble as shown without glue to check for fit and squareness. If you are satisfied, take the box apart and repeat with glue. When the glue is dry, remove the tape and sand the top and bottom edges square and even.

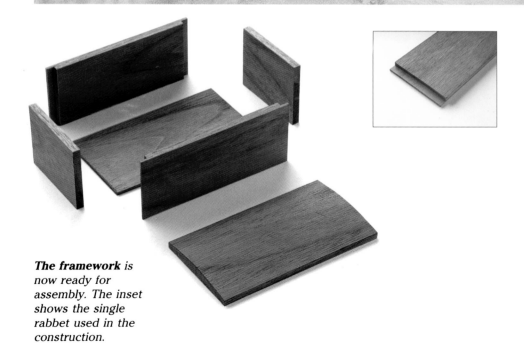

The framework is now ready for assembly. The inset shows the single rabbet used in the construction.

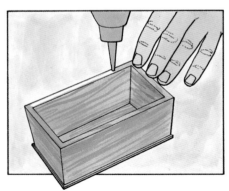

7 Sand the base smooth and glue it on, clamping gently. Glue and clamp the shaped lid to the rest of the framework. A wood block is used between the clamps and the lid to prevent the wood from being bruised when pressure is applied.

FITTING THE STRAP

To begin with, set the router to cut to a depth of less than $\frac{1}{32}$in or three-quarters of the depth of the banding. Set the distance from the fence to the near edge of the bit. Test the cut on a piece of scrap wood. If it is too loose, choose a narrower bit and proceed by sticking pieces of $\frac{1}{2}$in masking tape along the edge of the fence, gradually widening the cut to take the line. It is wise to leave the groove fractionally under-width, so that the line can be fitted to the groove.

8 Plane the ends, front and back, so that they are even and level. This is shown here being done by hand with a small block plane, but it could also be done with a powered disk sander.

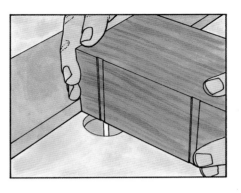

9 Having set up the router and fence as above, leave the tape in place and cut the grooves across the top and down each side of the back and front. Remove the tape and repeat the operation – the grooves should be just right!

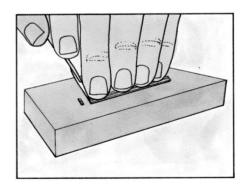

10 Cut the two pieces of banding for the lid about $\frac{1}{4}$in over-length and fit them accurately in the grooves, sanding the edges if necessary. Slightly undercutting the edges of the bandings helps to achieve a good, tight fit.

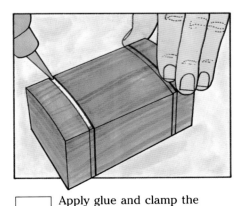

11 Apply glue and clamp the bandings in place using a curved piece of scrap wood. The curve is to match the curve of the lid of the trunk and the piece of scrap wood is again to prevent bruising. In this case, however, it also helps the clamp to seat more easily.

12 Cut the bandings for the front and back, again making them about $\frac{1}{4}$in over-length. The top end of each of these pieces must be cut at a slight angle so that they fit snugly under the pieces already in place. Glue, and, when dry, trim the ends flush (see illustration).

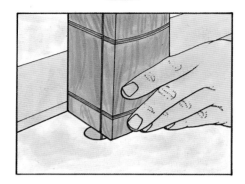

13	Bring the bandings down to the level of the rest of the box. This can be done initially with a sharp chisel, but is best finished with a cabinet scraper. Sand the whole box with 240-grit garnet paper.	*The box is now assembled* and the kingwood banding has been inlaid. The time has come to cut it open ready for fitting the lid.

14 Set up the router table with a $\frac{1}{16}$ in bit, cutting to a depth of $\frac{7}{32}$ in around the line that forms the base of the lid. With the *base* of the box against the fence, cut a groove right around the box.

FITTING THE HINGE

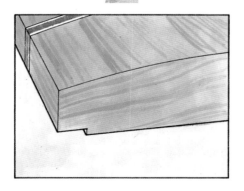

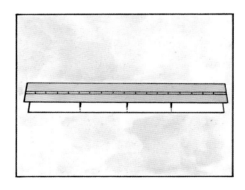

15 Use an X-ACTO or other sharp knife to cut through the final $\frac{1}{32}$ in and trim the rough edge with a chisel. Sand the two halves on a flat surface and check their fit to one another. Finish the surfaces now, while they are accessible (see pages 120-123).

16 Using two pieces of scrap wood to represent the lid and the box, cut a rabbet $\frac{1}{32}$ in deep and $\frac{1}{4}$ in wide along the back edge of the lid and framework to check that the hinge fits in the recess. Then cut a rabbet in the lid itself and box.

17 Cut a piece of the piano hinge to length and position it so the holes are centered end to end.

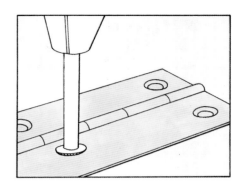

18 Mark carefully through the holes in the hinge onto the rabbet in the lid, and then drill and screw the hinge in place.

19 Mark through the *end holes only* onto the rabbet on the base – this is to allow for possible alterations. Drill these holes and screw the lid in place. Now close the lid. It should be a perfect fit, but it seldom is on the first attempt.

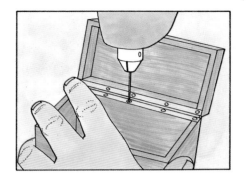

20 By drilling the remaining holes fractionally off-center, you can adjust the relative positions of the two halves. When you have the two halves lined up, drill any remaining holes dead center. Insert the screws and line up the screw heads in one direction for a finished look.

FITTING THE CATCH

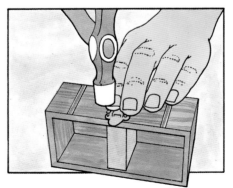

21 Place the complete catch in a central position and mark holes for the *bottom section only* at this stage to guarantee a perfect fit with the lid section later. Fit the bottom part of the lock in place, put the top part in position, mark, drill, and fit, using a supporting block (as shown).

The finished box *looking ready for travel. Inset detail shows the piano hinge.*

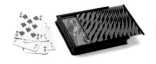

CARD BOX

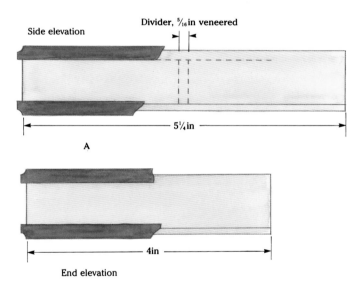

Section through A

⁷⁄₈ in

⁵⁄₁₆ in

¹⁄₈ in

Side elevation

Divider, ⁵⁄₁₆ in veneered

5¼ in

A

4 in

End elevation

This striking box will be the ideal place to keep your cards, whatever game you play.

The sliding mechanism gives the box added interest. It is achieved by the ebony molding, which forms a groove with the rabbet along the inside of the sides. Tiger-stripe veneer was used here, but many other colorful "composite" veneers are available from most veneer and marquetry suppliers. Try to buy "sample" pieces because whole sheets are expensive.

The interior is lined with figured maple veneer, and the contrast with the bubinga sides gives the box a feel of quality. If you have a particular set of cards in mind, you might like to choose your lid veneer to match – and check that the cards will fit the box as described here because cards specially designed for poker are wider.

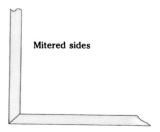

Mitered sides

CUTTING LIST

MAIN BOX

FRONT/BACK (bubinga 2 pieces)
$\frac{7}{8} \times \frac{5}{32} \times *5\frac{1}{2}$in

SIDES (bubinga 2 pieces)
$\frac{7}{8} \times \frac{5}{32} \times *4\frac{1}{4}$in

DIVIDER (bubinga 1 piece)
$*\frac{3}{4} \times \frac{5}{32} \times *4$in

LID (birch ply 1 piece)
$*4 \times \frac{1}{8} \times *5\frac{1}{4}$in

BASE (birch ply 1 piece)
$*4\frac{3}{16} \times \frac{1}{16} \times *5\frac{1}{4}$in

MOLDINGS (ebony 1 piece)
$4 \times \frac{1}{4} \times 6\frac{3}{8}$in

*Allowance for waste

VENEERS

(figured maple 1 piece)
6×18in

(tiger-stripe 1 piece)
$4\frac{1}{4} \times 11$in

TOOLKIT

For basic kit, see pages 8-13

Small paintbrush for applying glue

A veneer press or clamps and cauls

WOODS TO USE

When you make a box such as this, imagination is the keyword as there are so many exciting woods to choose from. Brazilian **MAHOGANY** or Australian **JARRAH** for the sides would look good. As for veneers, there are even more species to choose from. Something like **BLACK WALNUT** for the top would be more subtle, but still eye-catching.

PREPARING THE VENEER

1 First prepare the wood (see pages 16-21). Cut the pieces for the sides and the divider roughly to length. Tape a piece of the figured maple veneer big enough for the five pieces, apply glue, and place the pieces on it.

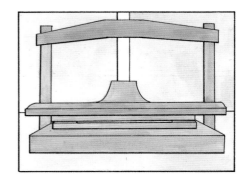

2 Put a sheet of paper, then a piece of carpet underlay, and finally a rigid board on top of the pieces. Put in a press or clamp with cauls.

PREPARING LID AND BASE

3 Cut the pieces for the lid and base roughly to size. Cut two pieces of the tiger-stripe veneer for the lid and two pieces of the figured maple for the base.

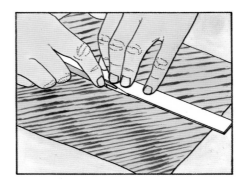

4 When the pieces for the sides and divider are dry, remove them from the press and veneer both sides of the lid and both sides of the base in the same way.

FRAMEWORK CONSTRUCTION

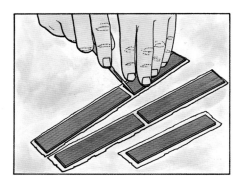

| **5** | Separate the pieces for the sides and divider, and carefully trim the excess veneer from them. Veneer the other side of the divider in the same way. |

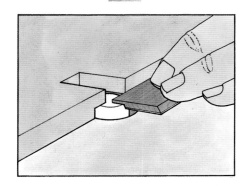

| **6** | Cut the miters (see page 27, step 1). Cut a rabbet $\frac{1}{8}$in high and $\frac{3}{16}$in wide along the top edge of the insides of the sides. |

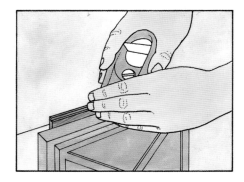

| **7** | Plane off the thin part of one end so that the piece is as high as the bottom of the rabbet of its neighboring sides. This is where the lid enters the box. |

A detail of a side
*ready for assembly,
showing the lid
rabbet and miter.*

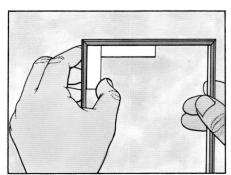

| **8** | Tape the pieces together to check for fit and squareness, and glue if you are satisfied. It is vital that the piece is absolutely square, because you will have problems with the sliding lid even if it is only slightly out of true. |

| **9** | Cut the base slightly over-size, sand smooth, and glue it to the bottom of the side assembly, making sure that the former is sanded completely even. Clamp gently. |

MAKING THE MOLDINGS

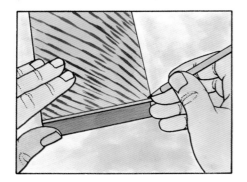

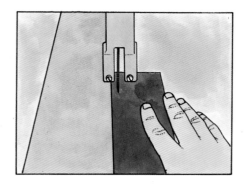

10 Unclamp when dry and pencil-mark the exact size of the finished lid. Plane the lid exactly to size; make sure it slides easily, but is not too loose. When it is in place, the back edge of the lid should be flush with the end. Sand thoroughly and apply a coat of sanding sealer.

11 Plane the $4 \times 6\frac{1}{2}$in piece of ebony to exactly $\frac{1}{4}$in thick and plane one edge square and straight.

12 Saw this off on a bandsaw set to $\frac{9}{32}$in and plane the new raw edge. Repeat until you have eight pieces – each should have three planed and one sawn edge. Plane the sawn edges until they are smooth and true.

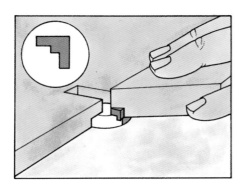

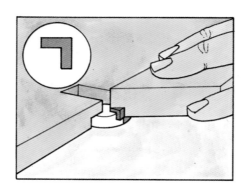

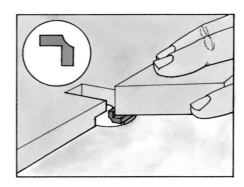

13 To rout the rabbet in these pieces, you need to hold them in a safety jig while working them. Set the bit to two-thirds of the final required height, but to the full depth. Using a safety jig (as above) make a cut in the first piece, reverse it end for end, and make another pass.

14 Now increase the height of the cutter to the required final measurement and do the third cut on all the pieces. This should produce the profile above.

15 Using a $\frac{9}{16}$in-diameter radius cutter, cut the curved section to produce the profile above. This must be carefully set up so that the profile is symmetrical. Use the other, plain edge of the safety jig to make these final cuts safely. The moldings are complete.

The framework is assembled and the moldings are completed ready for cutting to length and fitting.

FITTING THE MOLDINGS

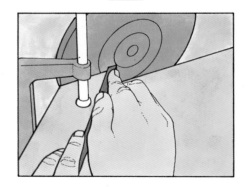

16 The miters are best done using the disk sander. Set up the sander as shown and work a 45-degree angle at one end of each piece. Reverse the jig and, starting at a bottom edge, hold a piece in position on the box with the 45-degree angle exactly in place at a corner.

17 Being sure to hold the molding as steady as possible, mark with a scriber at the other end on the inside of the molding.

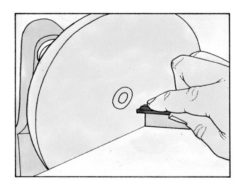

18 Cut roughly to length and work the miter on the sander, slowly working back toward the scribed line. This is a very accurate method of cutting miters on small pieces of wood.

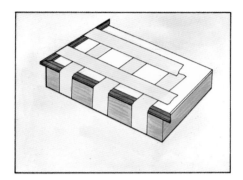

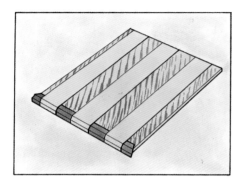

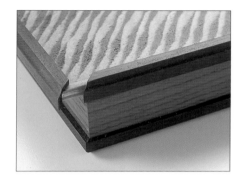

19 When you are satisfied, glue and tape the piece in place. Repeat with the next piece, working clockwise, and set it aside for the glue to set. When it is dry, remove the tape and repeat for the last two pieces around the base. Repeat for the three sides around the top.

20 Glue the fourth piece to the back of the lid, having positioned it accurately with the lid in place first. Finish those surfaces not already treated (see pages 120-123).

The inset shows a detail of the back of the sliding lid.

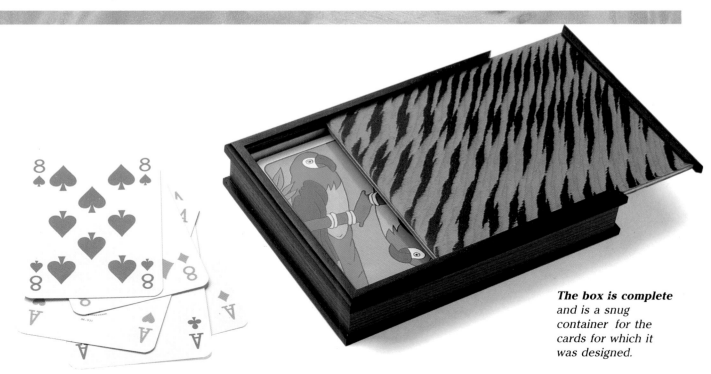

The box is complete and is a snug container for the cards for which it was designed.

PENCIL BOX

This pencil box, with its elegant, slim lines and ebony detail highlighting the rich, warm color of the yew, will enhance any desktop. It features a tilting lid that opens at a touch to reveal an interior in beautifully figured yew burl. The mitered corners are strengthened and decorated by matching ebony splines, and the lid is finished with a burled yew panel bordered with ebony.

Half section

5/16 in

1/8 in

3/16 in

3/16 in

Plan

8in

4in

1/16 in ebony veneer

1 1/8 in

1 3/4 in

Miter detail

End elevation

4in

Divider 3/16 in thick

1/16 in ebony veneer

1 1/16 in

A

A: The rabbet on the inside top edges tapers from 5/16 in to 3/16 in in the space of 2 1/4 in.

Side elevation

CUTTING LIST

MAIN BOX

FRONT/BACK (yew 2 pieces)
$1 \times \frac{5}{32} \times *8\frac{1}{16}$ in

SIDES (yew 2 pieces)
$1 \times \frac{5}{32} \times *4\frac{1}{4}$ in

DIVIDER (yew 1 piece)
$*\frac{9}{16} \times \frac{5}{32} \times *4$ in

LID (yew 2 pieces)
$*2 \times \frac{1}{8} \times *8$ in

BASE (birch ply 1 piece)
$*4 \times \frac{1}{8} \times *8$ in

*Allowance for waste

VENEERS

Two identical pieces $2\frac{1}{2} \times 8$ in, taken from two consecutive sheets of well-figured yew veneer, and one piece $4\frac{1}{4} \times 8$ in, 4 strips $\frac{1}{4}$ in-wide $\frac{1}{16}$ in ebony veneer

TOOLKIT

For basic kit, see pages 8-13

A veneer press or clamps and cauls

A small file

MATERIALS

Small brass pins

WOODS TO USE

EBONY and **YEW** are woods of extreme contrast, and this mixture of light and dark can be quite striking. A similar effect could be gained using **SYCAMORE** or **MAPLE** for the main body of the box and highlighting the detail with **WENGE** or brown **OAK**.

JOINTING THE LID

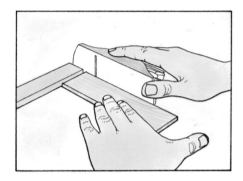

1 Plane one edge of one of the prepared pieces absolutely straight and square using a step and stop set-up (see pages 16-21). Plane one edge of the other piece, *but the other way up* to cancel out any error there may be in your set-up.

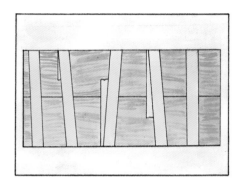

2 Put the two pieces together, and hold up to the light to check for openings. When you are satisfied, glue and tape these pieces together. If you remembered to reverse one piece during planing, they should go together completely flat.

PREPARING THE BASE

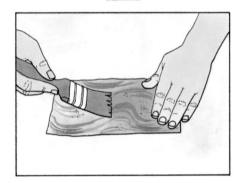

3 Select two well-figured and identically matched pieces from two consecutive sheets of burled yew veneer. A small mirror is a good way of checking a book-match. Cut out two pieces and a single piece for the bottom, dampen and place between paper under pressure.

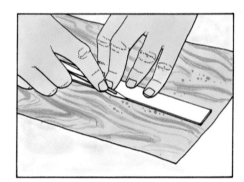

4 When the veneer is flat and dry (you may need to change the paper once), cut along one edge where you want the joint to be using a craft knife and straightedge, cutting the other piece in the same place to make sure it matches.

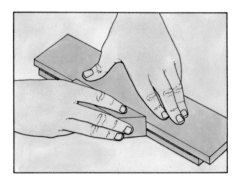

5 Tape the two pieces together and place them between two pieces of wood with just the merest sliver protruding. Use a piece of 240-grit garnet paper on a block to sand the edges even and ready for joining.

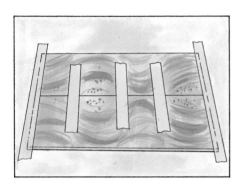

6 Tape one piece of veneer on a board with waxed paper under the edge to be joined to prevent it from sticking to the board. Put glue along the edge of the other piece, tape it in position, place a board over the top and either clamp or put it in a veneer press until the glue is dry.

7 Tape the veneer for the underneath of the base to a board with paper underneath. When the book-matched veneer is dry, apply glue. Put the ply for the base in place, apply more glue, and place the book-matched veneer on the top. Place in a press or clamp with cauls.

PREPARING THE SIDES

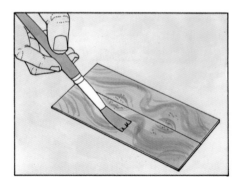

8 When it is dry, trim the veneer from the edges. Plane exactly to size, sand thoroughly, and check that it will fit snugly into a $\frac{3}{16}$in groove made in a piece of scrap. Give it a coat of thinned sanding sealer.

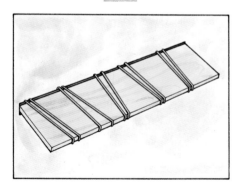

9 Cut five slightly over-length $\frac{1}{4}$in strips from the ebony veneer for the four sides and divider, and glue these into place along the top edges of all five pieces, the dimensions for which are given in the cutting list. Hold in place with rubber bands. Allow to dry.

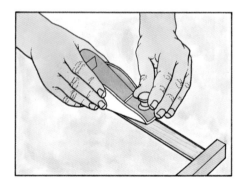

10 Remove the rubber bands and plane the edges of the ebony flush. Use a small block plane and work very carefully. Above all, make sure that the plane is razor-sharp.

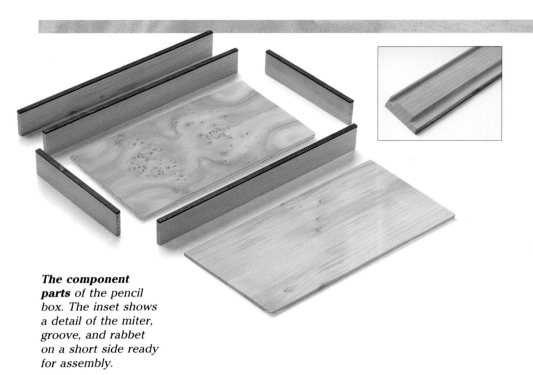

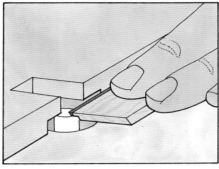

The component parts of the pencil box. The inset shows a detail of the miter, groove, and rabbet on a short side ready for assembly.

11 Cut the miters as shown on page 27, step 1, and then cut a rabbet $\frac{5}{64}$in deep and $\frac{3}{16}$in wide along the top inside edge of each of the long sides. Set the router to cut the same depth for the short sides, but $\frac{5}{16}$in wide.

ASSEMBLY

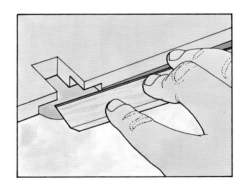

12 Using an angled piece of scrap wood as a jig, as shown above, make the diagonal cut at the end of each of the long sides to form the tilting mechanism.

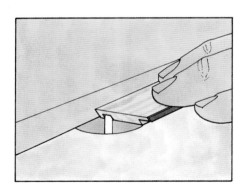

13 Cut a $\frac{3}{16}$in groove along the bottom edge of each side to accept the base, and sand the inside of each piece smooth.

14 To assemble the sides and base, wait until the base is dry, lightly sand with 1200 grit wet and dry paper and 0000 steel wool. Assemble the sides and base to check for fit and squareness. Then take apart and repeat the assembly with glue.

PREPARING THE LID

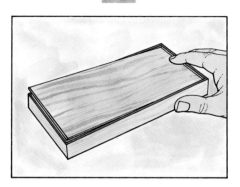

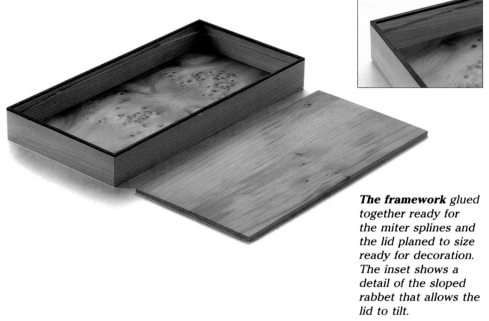

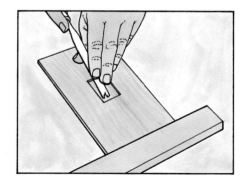

15 Remove the tape from the jointed lid and scrape gently to remove any glue. Sand until perfectly smooth. When the side and base assembly is set, remove the tape and measure accurately the required size for the lid, planing it to size. It should now tilt easily.

The framework glued together ready for the miter splines and the lid planed to size ready for decoration. The inset shows a detail of the sloped rabbet that allows the lid to tilt.

LID DECORATION

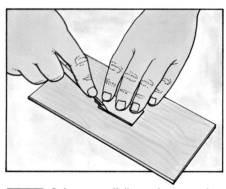

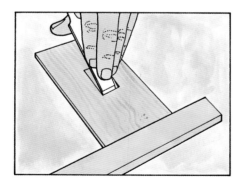

16 Select a well-figured piece of yew and flatten it as before. Cut a piece of $\frac{1}{16}$in birch plywood to $1\frac{3}{4} \times 1\frac{1}{8}$in, place it centrally on the lid, and cut around it with a craft knife.

17 Use a wide chisel to remove the wide just inside this cut. At this stage a mistake would be serious, so work deliberately and carefully.

18 Remove the rest of the wood with a very shallow gouge and clean up with a chisel held vertically and used as a scraper. The recess needs to be only $\frac{1}{32}$in or the thickness of your veneer.

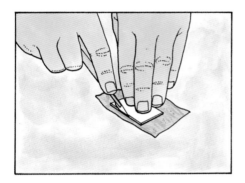

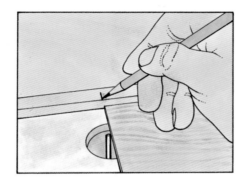

19 When the veneer for the panel is flat, cut out a piece using the $\frac{1}{16}$in ply as a template and glue it in position in the recess. This does not have to be accurate because the joint will be covered by the ebony border. When this is dry, scrape it even.

20 Make a mark on a piece of tape attached to the router fence squarely opposite the center of a $\frac{1}{16}$in straight bit. This must be done accurately.

21 Measure as shown above and set the distance from the fence to the *center* of the bit to this number. Measure the distance from the side of the lid to the nearest edge of the panel and *add* $\frac{3}{32}$in. Mark this distance on both sides of the fence's central mark.

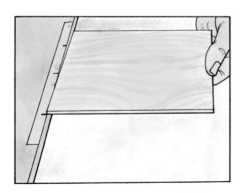

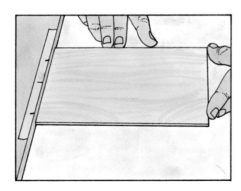

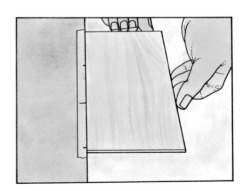

22 Turn the router on and place the end of the lid firmly against the fence, the right edge on the table, the left edge raised about $\frac{3}{16}$in and the left corner at the left marker on the fence.

23 Lower the lid onto the bit, making sure that the end is firmly against the fence, and move the lid to the left until the right edge is by the right marker. Lift the right edge from the table and the cut is done! Repeat for the other end.

24 Repeat for the long sides using appropriate measurements. You will need to check that your center mark is still accurate after you have moved the fence.

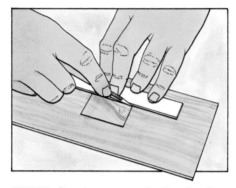

| 25 | Cut the corners by hand using a small straight edge, a craft knife, and a fine chisel. This is to square them up, because a router cutter leaves a curved corner. |

| 26 | Cut a piece of the ebony stringing to fit one of the grooves, mitering each corner using a chisel and a 45-degree block. Fit and glue in place. When set, chisel down to the level of the lid, scrape level, sand with 240, then 320 grit garnet paper and apply sealer. |

The lid detail
complete and looking very attractive.

INSTALLING THE DIVIDER

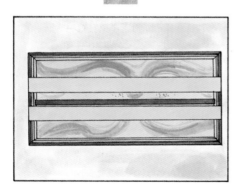

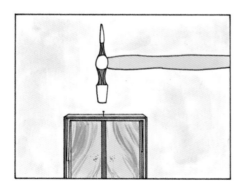

| 27 | Plane the divider to ½in, trim to length, and glue in place, making sure it is placed absolutely centrally. |

| 28 | Drill accurately through the sides into the ends of the divider using a drill bit that is slightly smaller than your pins. Hammer them three-quarters of the way in. |

| 29 | Cut off the heads with a jeweler's piercing saw, and file the projecting pins flush and smooth, making sure that you do not damage the sides of the box. |

EBONY MITER SPLINES

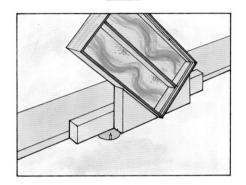

30 Use the router to cut the slots for the miter splines, using a $\frac{1}{16}$in straight cutter made from scrap and a spline jig as shown in the illustration above.

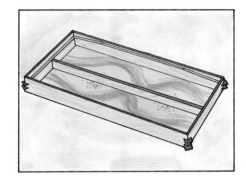

31 Glue in small pieces of $\frac{1}{16}$in ebony veneer with the grain running across the corners. Leave the ebony veneer to dry.

32 Cut off the surplus ebony using a piercing saw, and plane smooth, working away from the corners to avoid "break out," which can easily happen when the wood is thin and brittle. The box is now complete except for the finishing process (see pages 120-123).

These pens look at home in the finished box. The inset shows a detail of the ebony miter splines.

LAMINATED BOX

CUTTING LIST

MAIN BLOCK (Spanish olive 10 pieces)
*3 × $^9/_{32}$ × *4 in

MAIN BLOCK (Spanish olive 10 pieces)
*3 × $^1/_8$ × *4 in

*Allowance for waste

TOOLKIT

For basic kit, see pages 8-13

Bandsaw, fitted with $^1/_4$ in blade

Curved scraper

MATERIALS

For hinge pin, $^1/_{16}$ in brass rod or similar 2 in

WOODS TO USE

Any of the decorative hardwoods could be used for this project – **WALNUT, ANDAMAN PADAUK**, or **ROSEWOOD** for instance – either in a laminated form or from the solid. You may want to experiment with the design and try it in a good quality plywood first to get a feel for it.

This project is created out of a single block, laminated up from pieces of highly decorative Spanish olive and layers of dyed veneers.

This is a simple project to make, and if you prefer, it can be further simplified by starting with a single, solid piece of wood. .

The hinge pins used here are $^1/_{16}$ in in diameter. You could use larger ones – don't use smaller – but they must go into solid wood. A wide variety of gauges is available from non-ferrous metal suppliers. This size is on the border line of what is referred to as wire and rod. In any case, the first holes you drill should be very slightly less than the diameter of the pins, and the second holes should be the exact diameter.

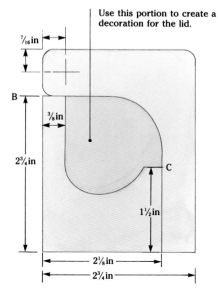

Use this portion to create a decoration for the lid.

End elevation

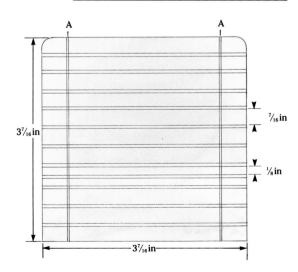

PREPARING THE BLOCK

First prepare your wood (see pages 16-21). It is not necessary to plane the edges or end grain absolutely to size at this stage, but each piece must be accurately flat ready for laminating.

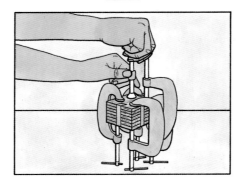

1 Make a black/blue/black "sandwich" of veneers large enough to yield eight pieces 3 × 4in and a black/red/black "sandwich" to yield three pieces the same size. When dry, cut the pieces to size, glue in the order shown in plan, and clamp firmly.

2 When the block is complete, remove the clamps and plane all the surfaces straight and square. Then carefully clean up the whole cube with fine sandpaper and a block.

The laminated block
completed, planed, and sanded, and ready to be bandsawn.

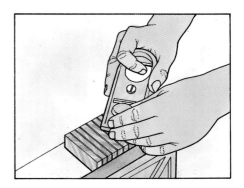

3 Set up a fence on your bandsaw to give a ½in cut and proceed to cut ½in off each side of the block. These cuts are shown clearly marked as A on the plan.

4 Plane off all the saw marks, making sure that you keep the new faces flat and straight. Remember that you are planing end grain, so always work *in* from the edges of the pieces to prevent the grain from breaking out.

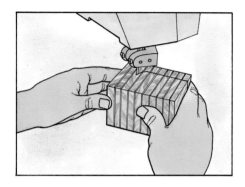

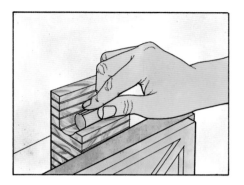

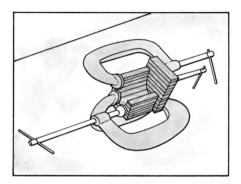

| 5 | Mark the shape of the lid on one side of the central block and cut this out on the bandsaw. This cut is marked B on the plan. |

| 6 | Mark and cut out the shape for the interior space from the remaining block. Scrape and sand all the new surfaces. Keep the waste portion for the lid decoration, which is shown by the crosshatched area on the plan. |

| 7 | Now glue the sides in place on the central block. For accuracy this is best done one side at a time, making sure that the bottom and back edges are flush with the central block. |

ATTACHING THE LID

The position of the holes for the lid hinge pins suits the plan as shown here. If you change the plan, the holes should enter the lid halfway through its thickness and the same distance from its back edge.

| 8 | Round over the lower back edge of the lid, either by hand or by using a $\frac{5}{16}$in corner-round bit in the router. Make sure you don't work on the wrong edge by mistake. |

| 9 | Tape the lid securely in place and drill a $\frac{1}{16}$in hole $\frac{3}{4}$in deep on each side at the point shown on the plan. Drill $\frac{1}{4}$in into these holes with a very slightly larger drill bit. This will ensure that the pins bind in the holes in the lid and won't work loose. |

10 Gently tap in the pins, taking care not to bend them. Use pliers to cut off the heads, then remove the tape and file the pins smooth until they are flush with the surface of the box.

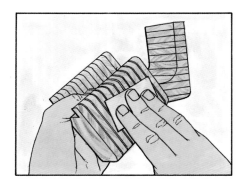

11 Round over all the top and side edges on the router using the $^5/_{16}$ in corner-round bit. Sand all surfaces smooth. Take a little time over this, as a good finish is very important.

12 Carve the waste portion to any shape that meets your fancy, and smooth it well. Remember to leave a flat base to give it a good gluing area, and glue it in place on the lid.

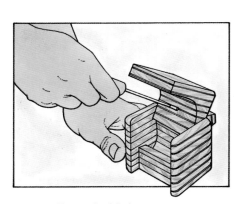

13 If you feel it is necessary, you can also screw it in place from underneath the lid. The screw head can be covered by setting the head in a deep hole, gluing in an olive plug, and smoothing it off later.

The finished box, resembling a modern sculpture as much as a box. The front swings out and up like a "gull-wing" door on a sports car to reveal a small, safe space inside.

HEXAGONAL BOX

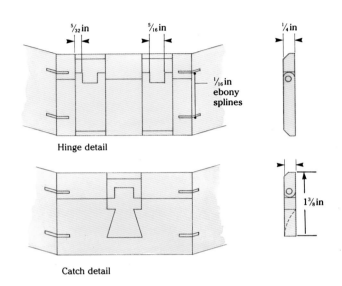

5/32 in   5/16 in   1/4 in

1/16 in ebony splines

Hinge detail

Catch detail

This unusual hexagonal box, in cocobolo, glass, and ebony, features an all-wood catch and hinges. You will need some 1/8 in hardwood dowel, which is available from lumberyards, and an appropriately sized drill bit so that the dowel fits snugly with only light sanding.

Because it is difficult to drill really accurate vertical holes in small pieces of wood, the pieces for the hinges are drilled using a small drill stand while they are still over-size and then planed down toward the hole.

The sides are mitered at 60 degrees, which produces an angle between adjacent sides of 120 degrees. Some miter saws have a 60-degree setting marked; alternatively, you can make a 60-degree template from an equilateral triangle. Whichever way you usually cut miters, there will be a way of adapting it, so experiment on pieces of scrap wood. Do not order the glass until you have made the template. You can then be sure that it will fit the box you are actually making rather than the one in the plan, from which it may differ.

The distance between the two pieces of glass depends on what you want to use the space for. Here, planings from various pieces of laminated dyed veneers have been used.

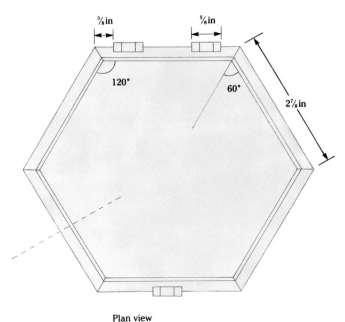

3/8 in   5/8 in

120°   60°

2 7/8 in

Plan view

Section

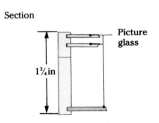

Picture glass

1 3/4 in

MAKING THE FRAMEWORK

CUTTING LIST

SIDES (cocobolo 6 pieces)
**2 × ⁵⁄₁₆ × *3in

HINGES (ebony 1 piece)
*1½ × ⁵⁄₁₆ × *¾in

HINGES (ebony 1 piece)
*1½ × ⁵⁄₁₆ × *1½in

CATCH (ebony 1 piece)
*¾ × ⁵⁄₁₆ × *¾in

CATCH (ebony 1 piece)
*¾ × ⁵⁄₁₆ × *1¼in

**Allowance for cutting off the lid
*Allowance for waste

TOOLKIT

For basic kit, see pages 8-13

¹⁄₁₆in straight bit

¹⁄₁₆in straight bit (or to suit glass)

Drill bit to fit ⅛in dowel

Pencil marking gauge

MATERIALS

⅛in hardwood dowel, maple, or similar, 3in

3 pieces ¹⁄₁₆in picture glass,
as template

Decorative "filling" for lid

WOODS TO USE

Good choices would be **BUBINGA** or **OLIVE**,
while **LEMONWOOD** has an even, light
color. The hinges and catch must be made
from a hard, dense wood, such as
LIGNUM VITAE.

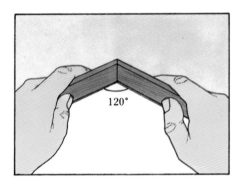

1 Prepare the wood (see pages 16-21). Now test on scrap wood that your chosen method of mitering produces a perfect 120-degree joint. Measure the six prepared pieces and cut a miter at each end of each piece to bring them to exactly the right length.

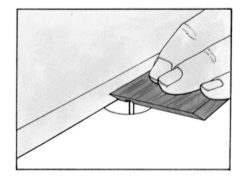

2 To take the glass base and the double layer lid, cut grooves ³⁄₃₂in deep as shown on the plan.

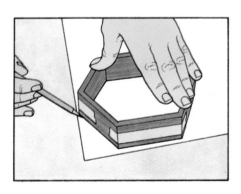

3 Tape the pieces together and draw around the shape on a piece of posterboard; cut out.

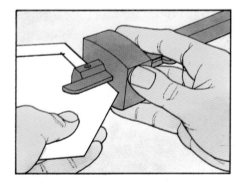

4 Using a pencil marking gauge, mark a line ⁷⁄₃₂in in from each of the outside edges and cut these portions off. This is the template for the glass and now is the time to get the three pieces cut.

The six sides and *three pieces of glass, cut and ready for assembly.*

| 5 | Assemble the box with the glass, but don't glue it until it all fits together comfortably. |

Disassemble and place one piece of glass in front of you, put your chosen filling – dried leaves or grasses, for example – on the glass. Place the other sheet on top.

INSTALLING SPLINES

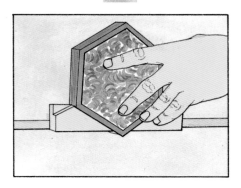

| 6 | Tape one double edge together and place the opposite edge in the double slot of one side of the box. Put the piece for the base in the other slot. |

| 7 | Glue all joints and wrap the sides around the pieces of glass, removing the tape holding the glass together as you go. Tape securely across the top and bottom of each miter. |

| 8 | To fit the splines, work as shown but use an improvised 120-degree spline jig, which will hold the box at the correct angle while you make the passes over the router bit (as shown above). |

CUTTING OFF LID

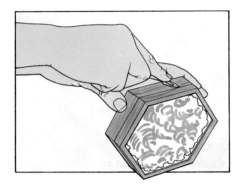

9 Cut off the lid using a $\frac{1}{16}$in router bit in the router table. Remember not to go all the way through, but cut the last $\frac{1}{32}$in with a craft knife.

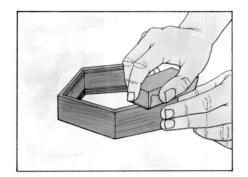

10 Trim and level all the newly exposed edges, first with a sharp chisel; then by working the pieces on a sheet of 240-grit garnet paper laid on a flat surface. Finally smooth with the grain using 240 and then 320-grit garnet on a small block. Sand all external surfaces smooth.

HINGES AND CATCH

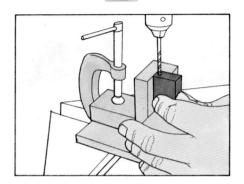

11 Drill a $\frac{1}{8}$in hole right through each of the four prepared ebony pieces, going across the grain as shown on the plan, $\frac{3}{32}$in from the end. Do this as accurately as you can, using a drill stand and jig to hold the pieces vertical.

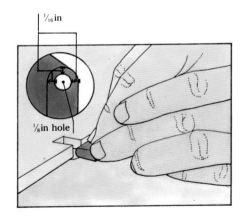

12 By careful planing, reduce the dimensions of the pieces to $\frac{1}{4}$in thick so the hole is *exactly* $\frac{1}{16}$in from each edge and the end at both sides. Round over the corners around the holes with a $\frac{1}{8}$in corner-round bit, or by chiseling and sanding.

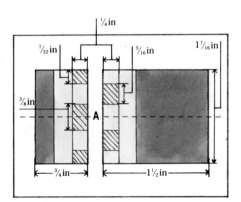

13 Accurately mark out the interlocking parts of the knuckle on the two pieces for the hinges. This is best done on masking tape if you are using ebony, because marks on such dark woods are hard to see.

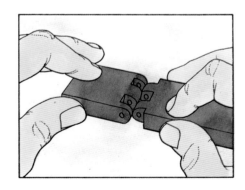

14 Cut down just inside the lines using a dovetail saw, and carefully chisel out the waste. Ebony is a very hard and often brittle wood, so work it with care. Trim until the pieces fit neatly together.

15 Join the halves with the dowel. It may need light sanding first, and a little wax will stop it from creaking! Saw in half along line A (see plan), plane the edges straight, and you have your two hinges.

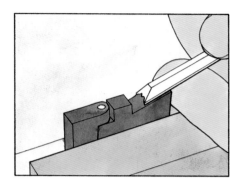

16 Repeat the operation for the catch. The bottom flap will need to be cut to the shape in the plan. Undercut the back of this flap behind the bottom to make it easy to open the box.

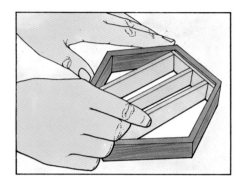

17 Use scrap wood to improvise a form for the inside of the lid and the box. The form will support the pressure while you clamp the hinges and catch in place, and help to avoid any distortion.

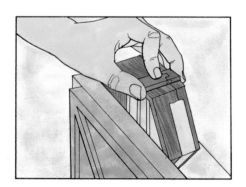

18 Tape the box together and place it in a vice with the back edge upward. Place a hinge so that its edge is 3/8in in from a corner and the "pin" is exactly level and square with the lid joint.

19 Hold the hinge firmly in place and cut around it gently with a craft knife. Remove the hinge and reinforce the lines with the knife, and repeat for the other hinge at the other end of the back edge.

20 Carefully cut out the recesses for the hinges, exactly 1/8in deep. When both fit snugly, glue and clamp in place, being careful not to get any glue on the moving parts.

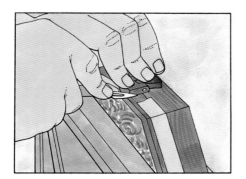

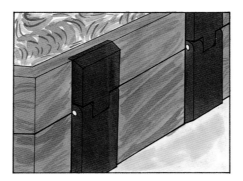

21 Remove the clamps and replace the box in the vice with its front upward. Cut the recess for the catch in the same way, but with the whole knuckle housed in the lid (see the plan). Glue and clamp in place, but only to the lid!

22 Chamfer the top and bottom edges of both hinges and the top of the catch, and the box is finished.

Hinge detail showing the all wooden construction in ebony with hardwood dowels used in the knuckles.

The finished box with a subtle display of laminated and dyed veneers used as the infill.

DISPLAY CASE

This shelf or wall-mounted case is designed to be placed at, or just below, eye-level, and the compartments are deeper than those of a traditional printer's type tray for the safety of the items displayed in it. The dimensions could, of course, be adjusted at the design stage to suit your own individual needs. It is best that the wood used for the main framework is plain and relatively unfigured. If you use a different profile for your moldings, remember that the thickness of the side derives directly from the width of these moldings, and adjust the plan as necessary.

CUTTING LIST

TOP/BOTTOM (cherry 2 pieces)
$1\frac{3}{4} \times \frac{1}{2} \times 13\frac{1}{2}$in

SIDES (cherry 2 pieces)
$1\frac{3}{4} \times \frac{1}{2} \times 9\frac{3}{4}$in

MAIN DIVIDER (cherry 1 piece)
*$1\frac{3}{4} \times \frac{1}{2} \times$ *$9\frac{1}{4}$in

VERTICAL DIVIDERS (cherry 4 pieces)
$1\frac{1}{2} \times \frac{5}{32} \times$ *9in

HORIZONTAL DIVIDERS
(cherry 8 pieces)
$1\frac{1}{2} \times \frac{5}{32} \times$ *$6\frac{1}{2}$in

MOLDINGS (cocobolo 1 piece)
$2 \times \frac{1}{2} \times 14\frac{1}{8}$in

EDGE BANDINGS (cocobolo 1 piece)
$2 \times \frac{3}{16} \times 10$in

BACK (birch plywood 1 piece)
*$9\frac{1}{2} \times \frac{1}{8} \times$ *14in

*Allowance for waste

Front elevation

X

A

2in

$1\frac{5}{8}$in

$9\frac{3}{4}$in

$14\frac{1}{4}$in

Y

*

Detail of construction

X
Y

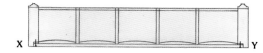

* Detail of miter joint for molding

Detail of construction

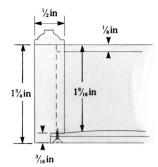

$\frac{1}{2}$in

$\frac{1}{8}$in

$1\frac{3}{4}$in

$1\frac{9}{16}$in

$\frac{3}{16}$in

TOOLKIT

For basic kit, see pages 8-13

$\frac{3}{16}$in straight bit

$\frac{3}{8}$in or larger straight bit

$\frac{1}{8}$in radius corner-round bit with guide pin/ball bearing

3 small bar clamps, opening at least 15in

Rubber bands

Countersink bit

MATERIALS

A piece of $\frac{1}{8}$in foam rubber, $9\frac{1}{2} \times 14$in

A piece of fabric of your choice, $9\frac{1}{2} \times 14$in

30 $\frac{1}{2}$in no. 3 countersunk woodscrews

WOODS TO USE

WALNUT, MAPLE, or **YEW** would all be appropriate woods for the main framework, while **EBONY, ROSEWOOD,** or **KINGWOOD** could be used for the moldings and edge bandings to good effect. It is best that the woods you use contrast with one another.

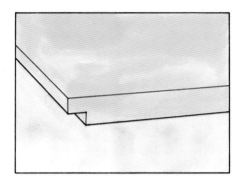

1 Prepare the wood (see pages 16-21). Cut a rabbet at each end of the pieces for the top and bottom to produce a tongue $\frac{1}{4} \times \frac{1}{4}$in, plus a $\frac{1}{4}$in groove to accommodate these $\frac{1}{4}$in from the end of each of the sides.

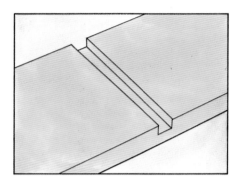

2 Now cut a $\frac{1}{2}$in groove (or dado as it is sometimes called) halfway along the inside edge of the top and bottom to take the main central divider. This is also $\frac{1}{4}$in deep.

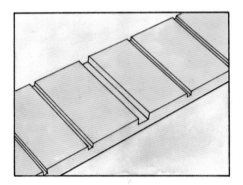

3 Accurately mark the position of the far left vertical divider on the front edge of the piece you are going to use for the top.

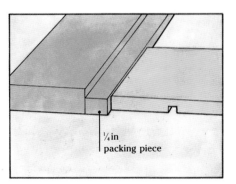

$\frac{1}{4}$in
packing piece

4 Using a $\frac{3}{16}$in straight bit and the right-angle miter gauge, cut this groove $\frac{3}{16}$in deep. Repeat for both ends of the top and bottom, and reset the fence for all the other grooves. Use a $\frac{1}{4}$in block against the fence for the main central divider.

MOLDINGS AND BANDINGS

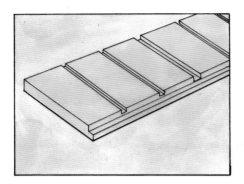

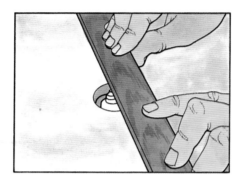

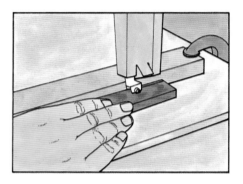

5 Cut a rabbet all the way along the back inside edge of the top and bottom, and one stopping ¼in from the end of the sides. Cut the end of the rabbet square by hand, because it will have been left curved by the router bit. Sand all surfaces smooth.

6 Cut along one edge of the prepared piece of cocobolo using a ⅛in radius corner-round bit with guide pin/ball bearing to produce half the required profile. Turn the piece over and repeat the process to complete the profile.

7 Bandsaw this piece off and repeat until you have the five pieces required to form the decorative edge bandings for the sides and center divider. Plane the sawn edges smooth using a plane clamped upside-down in a vice and drawing the pieces along it.

MAKING THE DIVIDERS

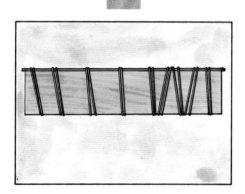

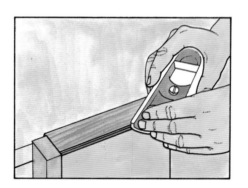

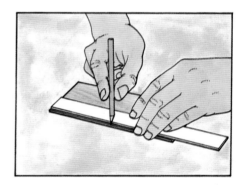

8 Cut 12 strips ¼in wide from the piece of cocobolo prepared for edge banding the small dividers and glue these in place, holding them in position with rubber bands until the glue is dry.

9 When dry, trim the ends square and plane flush using a small block plane. Lightly sandpaper them, taking care not to discolor the cherry with cocobolo dust, which is difficult to remove.

10 Accurately mark the intersection point A at the top end of the first vertical divider, remembering to allow the 3⁄16in that fits into the groove in the main framework.

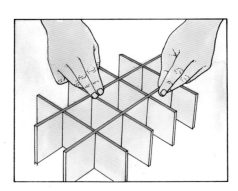

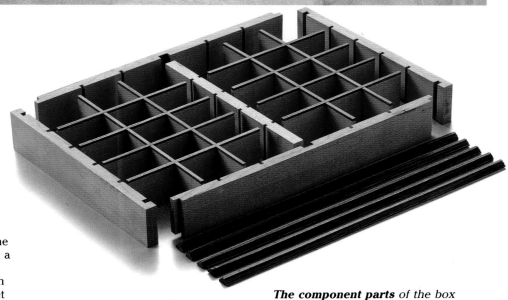

11 Cut the slot with a $^3/_{16}$ in bit and the right-angle miter gauge, cutting in a little more than halfway from the front (edge-banded) edge. Repeat for both ends of the four vertical dividers and reset the fence for each slot. Make cuts for the horizontal dividers from the back (non-edge-banded) edge and assemble.

The component parts of the box ready for assembly.

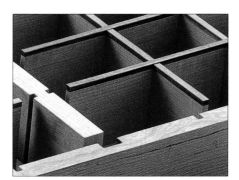

A detail of the dividers ready for slotting into the main framework. Notice the tight joints where the horizontal and vertical dividers cross.

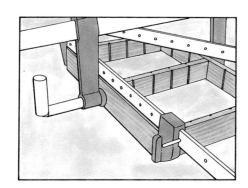

12 Now assemble the five pieces of the main framework without glue to check for fit and squareness. Take apart and adjust as necessary. When you are satisfied, reassemble with glue and clamp with bar clamps or similar.

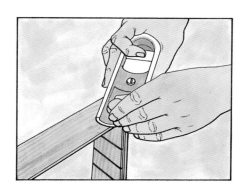

13 When the five pieces of the main framework are dry, plane the top and bottom edges flush, again using a small block plane, which must be razor-sharp and finely set.

INSTALLING MOLDINGS

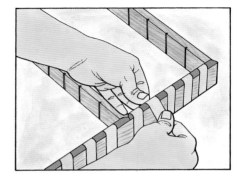

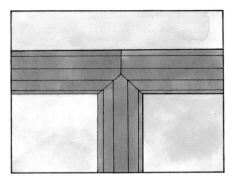

14 Cut the piece of molding for the top edge in half, square the matching ends on the disk sander and then, with the sander fence set at 45 degrees, form a miter halfway across the squared, matched end of each piece.

15 Form a full miter at the opposite end of the pieces, trimming exactly to length. Repeat for the bottom edge. Glue and tape in place.

16 Now cut a piece slightly over-length for the central divider and form a double miter at one end. Work the other end in the same way until it fits snugly. Glue and tape in place. Cut the pieces for the two sides, miter, glue, and tape them in place.

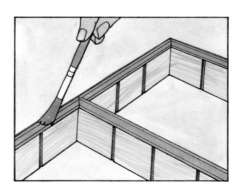

17 When dry, clean, sand carefully, and give all exterior surfaces and the front edges of the disassembled dividers a coat of thinned sanding sealer.

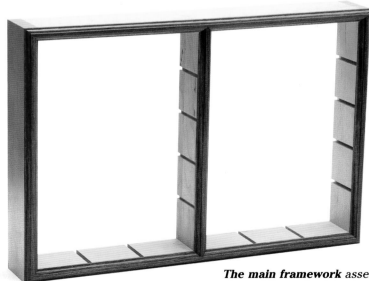

The main framework assembled with the moldings glued in place. Note the double miters on the moldings at each end of the central divider.

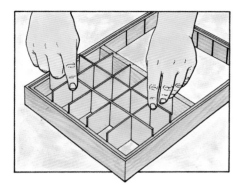

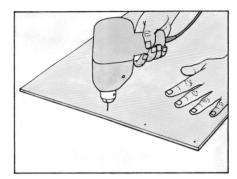

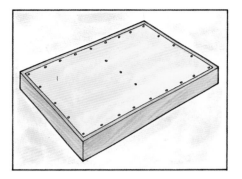

18 Sand the exterior surfaces smooth with 1200-grit wet and dry paper and 0000 steel wool and wax. Clean away any glue from the grooves under the moldings, reassemble the two sets of dividers, and slot them into place from behind the framework.

19 Cut a piece of $\frac{1}{8}$in birch plywood to size for the back, drill, and countersink this ready for installing.

20 Glue a sheet of $\frac{1}{8}$in foam rubber, and then a piece of fabric of your choice, to the inside of the board, using spray adhesive or similar. Screw the backboard in place, and the cabinet is ready to sit on a shelf or to be wall-mounted using mirror plates.

The finished display case, an attractive alternative to an old-fashioned printer's type tray. The fabric and foam pushed forward by the screwed-on backboard gives a luxurious padded feel to the back of the individual compartments.

DOVETAIL DESK BOX

CUTTING LIST

MAIN BOX

FRONT/BACK (American white oak 2 pieces)
**$3\frac{1}{16} \times \frac{3}{8} \times 11$in

SIDES (American white oak 2 pieces)
**$3\frac{1}{16} \times \frac{3}{8} \times 8\frac{1}{8}$in

LID (birch ply 1 piece)
*$4\frac{1}{2} \times \frac{5}{32} \times$ *$10\frac{5}{8}$in

BASE (American white oak 3 pieces)
*$3 \times \frac{1}{4} \times$ *$10\frac{5}{8}$in

TRAY

FRONT/BACK (cherry 2 pieces)
$1 \times \frac{5}{32} \times$ *$10\frac{1}{8}$in

SIDES (cherry 2 pieces)
$1 \times \frac{5}{32} \times$ *$7\frac{1}{4}$in

LONG DIVIDER (cherry 1 piece)
$\frac{3}{4} \times \frac{5}{32} \times$ *10in

SHORT DIVIDERS (cherry 3 pieces)
$\frac{3}{4} \times \frac{5}{32} \times$ *2in

BASE (cherry 3 pieces)
*$2\frac{3}{8} \times \frac{5}{32} \times$ *$10\frac{1}{8}$in

**Allowance for cutting off the lid
*Allowance for waste

Dovetail joints are decorative and very strong, both in their actual structure and the increased gluing surface they generate. The word dovetail, however, seems to strike fear into the hearts of woodworkers everywhere, although the difficulty is generally in the accurate laying out of the joint rather than in the cutting.

Use a sharp scriber and marking gauge and, above all, take your time. The size of the pins should be no more than half the size of the ends of the tails as measured on the front face. Remember to allow $\frac{1}{8}$ inch extra for the top complete pin to allow for the waste when the lid is cut off.

The colorful bandings that border the Canadian maple veneered lid are made by bandsawing strips off a "plank" made from colored veneers stacked and glued to produce the desired pattern. If you want to make your own individual bandings, see pages 97-103. Otherwise, choose from the many bandings available from veneer suppliers.

The quadrant hinges used here are a sturdy, attractive and practical alternative to ordinary butt hinges, and the integral stay automatically stops the lid at 90 degrees. It is important that the thickness of the sides of the box should be exactly the distance from the center of the pin to the edge of the main flap of your chosen hinges.

The simple and functional pen tray has four small compartments for thumb-tacks, paper clips, erasers, and the like. The pinned miters are strong and attractive, and the tray lifts out to reveal a green moire-lined space for those special letters and papers.

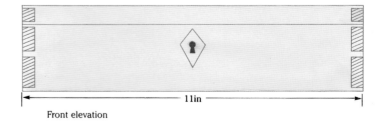

Front elevation

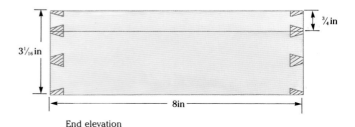

End elevation

Plan of tray

Dividers equally spaced

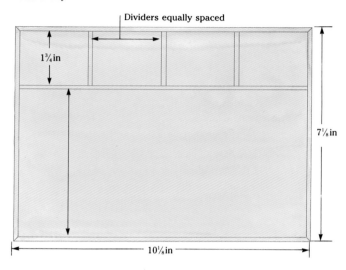

1¾ in

7⅛ in

10⅛ in

Joint detail

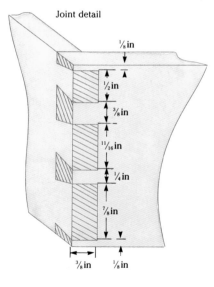

⅛ in

½ in

⅜ in

11/16 in

¼ in

⅞ in

⅜ in   ⅛ in

Tray joint detail

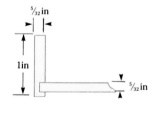

5/32 in

1 in

5/32 in

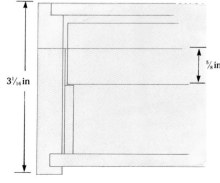

3 1/16 in

⅝ in

Section

TOOLKIT

For basic kit, see pages 8-13

3/16 in straight bit

½ in straight bit

¼ in brad point drill bit

Sliding bevel

¼ in bevel-edged chisel

⅛ in chisel

Round, flat, and triangular needle files

Short or right-angle chisel

Veneer press or boards, clamps and cauls

MATERIALS

A pair of small brass quadrant hinges

A small, good-quality brass box lock

Abalone or similar for the escutcheon

Fine brass pins, ½ in long

Thin fabric, green moire or similar, about 16 × 32in

Thin poster board 12 × 28in

Masonite, ⅛ in, two pieces 1¼ × 8in

Double-sided tape, 2in and ½ in

Decorative banding 3ft

WOODS TO USE

AUSTRALIAN SILKY OAK would work well, as would **QUEENSLAND MAPLE** or **ENGLISH ELM**.

DOVETAIL JOINTS

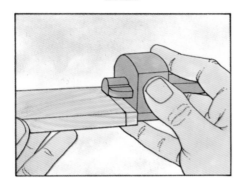

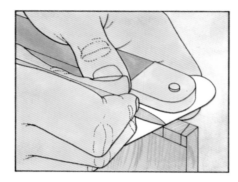

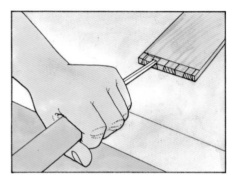

1 First prepare the wood (see pages 16-21). Mark ⅜in around each end of all four pieces for the sides on both faces and top and bottom edges. Mark the *outside* dimensions of the pins on the outer faces of the pieces for the front and back.

2 Mark across the end grain, using a sliding bevel set at an angle of 1:5 from 90 degrees, and continue these lines down the inside faces. Crosshatch the area to be removed.

3 Cut just inside the lines of one piece. Remove waste with the chisel blade on the original line marked around the end. Work in from each face. Repeat at both ends of front and back. Hold the piece vertically in a vice and trim back to the lines.

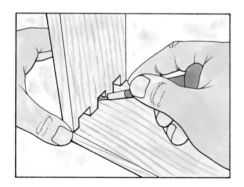

4 Position the end of one of the worked pieces against the inside face of one of the side pieces and line up the inside edge. Mark the position of the tails from the inside and continue the lines across the end grain. Repeat and number all four joints.

5 Remove the waste with a narrow chisel. Trim until it fits and repeat for all four joints. Veneer the plywood on both sides with the maple. Joint the pieces for the base, plane flush, and sand.

The four dovetailed sides, top and bottom of the box. Note how the dovetails vary in size, which adds greatly to the visual interest.

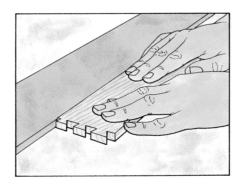

6 Cut a $\frac{3}{16}$in groove $\frac{1}{8}$in from the bottom of the inside faces of the four sides. Do not cut to the full length. Cut a rabbet $\frac{1}{4}$in deep by $\frac{1}{4}$in along the inside top edge of each piece, again not to the full length.

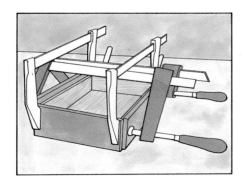

7 Cut the base to size and assemble. Glue using scraps of wood to make sure that the clamp pressure is directly on the tails at the sides and pins at the front and back. Prepare a complete piece for each of the sides to achieve this.

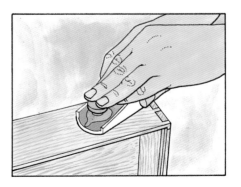

8 When the assembled box is dry, plane and sand the dovetailed corners. Cut the incomplete ends of the rabbets square with a chisel and then cut the lid exactly to size, then glue and clamp it in place. Plane the top edges of all sides flush.

DECORATIVE BANDINGS

The box glued together with the dovetails neatly assembled and the top and bottom in place.

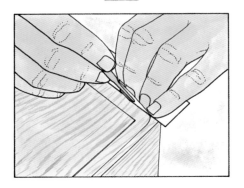

9 Cut a channel along the outside edges to cover the joint and to accommodate the decorative banding. You may need to make two cuts to get the size right. Test on scrap wood first. These must of course be incomplete passes with the corners trimmed square by hand.

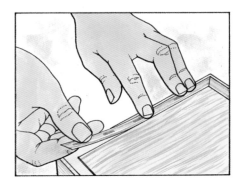

10 Now cut a length of your chosen banding, miter each end, and glue it in place. Repeat until the decoration is complete, and set aside to dry. When it is dry, scrape it even and give the lid a coat of sanding sealer.

| **11** | Use a $\frac{1}{16}$ in straight bit to make a groove all around the outside $\frac{3}{4}$ in from the top as |

deep as the bit will go to separate the lid. Do not cut through. Cut the rest of the way with a tenon saw. Wedge open where you have sawn, then plane.

The box after the lid has been cut off from the main framework.

INSTALLING HARDWARE

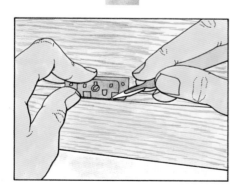

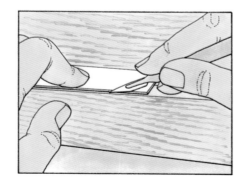

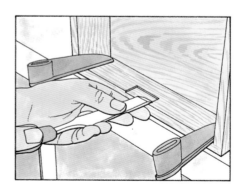

| **12** | Place the lock upside down, with the plate at the back, on the inside of the front edge of |

the box so that the *keyhole*, not the lock itself, will be exactly in the center.

| **13** | Remember that you will have reversed left for right because it is upside down. Hold it |

firmly in place and cut around it gently with a craft knife. Remove the lock and reinforce the lines with the knife and steel straight edge.

| **14** | Cut the lock in flush. Clamp the box, front down, and mark lines square down the inside |

face of the front from the ends of the portion already removed and mark the height of the lock. Remove this portion to the depth of the backplate.

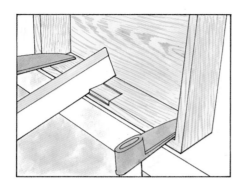

15 Mark the width of the working portion on the newly exposed wood and cut down to these lines. Go as deep as you can without cutting into the edge for the front of the lock. Remove this portion, cutting it square at the back with a chisel.

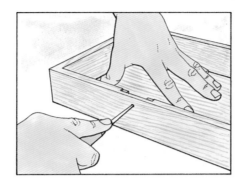

16 Measure where the center of the key should be and drill through from the outside using a drill smaller than the diameter of the key. The lock should fit snugly. View from the front to check that the hole is central and file to keyhole shape.

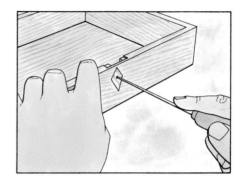

17 Cut the abalone to shape and sand the edges smooth. Hold it centrally over the keyhole, cut around with a craft knife and remove this portion to the depth of the abalone. Glue the abalone in place. When dry, even it up, drill for the keyhole, and shape with needle files.

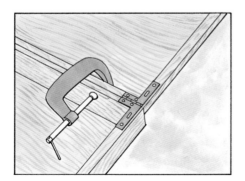

18 Clamp the back edges of the box and lid together. Remove the stays from the quadrant hinges by filing off one of the studs that hold them captive. Position the hinges so that the stay arms are flush with the inside edges of the sides; mark around each with a craft knife.

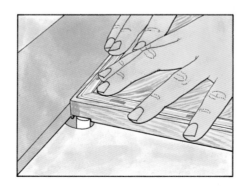

19 Take the width of the stay arm from the width of the side and set the fence this far away from a $\frac{1}{2}$in bit. Height is half the hinge-knuckle thickness. Hold back edges against the fence and cut in at each back corner of the lid and box to the ends of the stays.

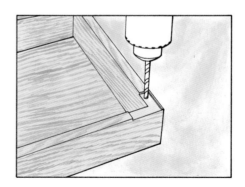

20 Work freehand on the router table to remove the waste to accommodate the main section of the hinges. Position hinges in their recesses and mark both ends of each of the small stay slots. Drill, on the box only, a $1\frac{5}{8}$in deep, vertical hole at each of these points.

MAKING THE TRAY

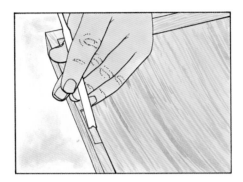

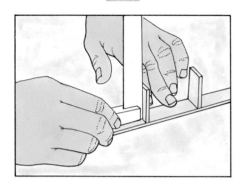

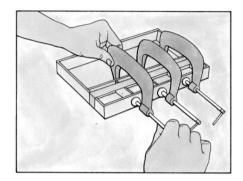

21 Angle drill and gouge to house the stays, and drill shallow holes for the top portion into the lid. Drill for lock and hinges, fix in place, and lock the top plate into the lock. Close the lid to register its position, and fit in place.

22 Joint the pieces for the tray base, plane to $\frac{5}{32}$ in, and cut to size. Miter the pieces for the sides, make a groove to take the base, and assemble. Cut the main divider to size and glue the three small dividers to it, spacing them evenly and checking for squareness.

23 When dry, pin the dividers in place (see page 50, steps 27-29), and glue them in place at the back of the tray. When they are dry, finish pinning, including the miters. Use two pins in the front and back and one from each side at each corner. Sand and seal.

LINING THE BOX

Only proceed with the lining when the finishing is complete (see pages 114-123). The box is lined by accurately covering cut pieces of poster board with fabric and attaching them. The amount by which you will need to reduce the dimensions of each piece of poster board will vary, depending on the thickness of your fabric – experiment. Prepare the poster board by sticking 2in-wide double-sided tape to one side to cover it completely.

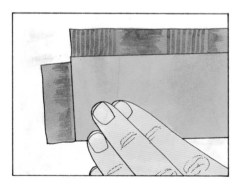

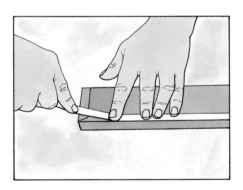

24 Cut two pieces of poster board each $\frac{3}{64}$ in shorter and $\frac{1}{32}$ in less high than the internal length and height of the main box respectively. Stick one piece to the reverse side of a piece of the fabric, leaving about $\frac{3}{8}$ in on one long and both short sides. Cut the corners as shown.

25 Stick $\frac{1}{2}$ in double-sided tape to the poster board down each of the short sides, and stick down the end flaps. Put another length of tape along the top edge of the poster board, and stick down the flap. Stick in place in the back of the box; repeat for the front.

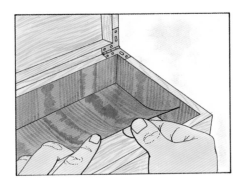

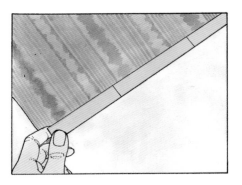

26 Measure for the poster board for the left side. Cut a piece of $\frac{1}{8}$in masonite the same length, but $\frac{5}{8}$in less high than this piece. Position it at the bottom of the taped side of the board, cut along the top edge, remove the backing, and stick in place.

27 Cover the whole piece with fabric as before. Slit the waste fabric by the step so it lies flat. Repeat for the right side and stick both in place. Measure for the base and cover as before. Stick in place.

28 Measure the inside of the lid and subtract $\frac{1}{16}$in from the sides and back and $\frac{3}{32}$in from the front. Make all pieces $\frac{1}{32}$in less wide. Cut and mark each piece. Stick them to the fabric, working left to right in the order: left, back, right, front.

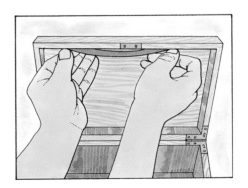

29 Cut to allow $\frac{3}{8}$in along the top edge and at each end. Apply double-sided tape and fold and secure as before. Stick in place in the order in which the pieces of poster board were laid on the fabric. Line the underneath of the lid as with the base of the box.

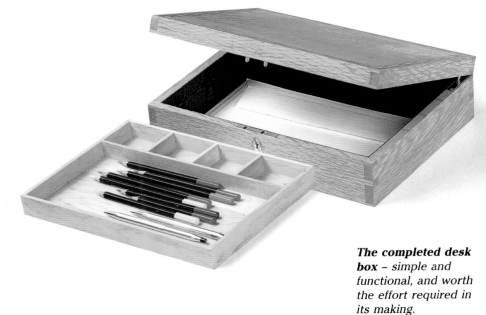

The completed desk box – simple and functional, and worth the effort required in its making.

OVAL BOX

TOOLKIT

For basic kit, see pages 8-13

$\frac{1}{8}$in slot cutter or to suit decorative inlay

$\frac{1}{8}$in radius corner-round bit with guide pin/ball bearing

---

Hollow plane (optional)

Curved scraper

Oval template – a rectangle of thin sheet brass with an oval 2 × $1\frac{1}{4}$in cut out of it. Long and short axes must be marked

---

A $\frac{3}{64}$in-wide scraper made from a piece of hacksaw blade or similar material for use with the above

---

Strong rubber bands

MATERIALS

Blue-dyed veneer 10 × 6in

Horse chestnut or holly veneer 2 × $1\frac{3}{4}$in

Red-dyed veneer 2 × $\frac{3}{8}$in

$\frac{1}{8}$in decorative inlay, as plan, 4ft long

$\frac{3}{64}$in black/white/black inlay, $5\frac{1}{2}$in long

---

$\frac{1}{2}$in brass piano hinge $4\frac{1}{4}$in long

---

10 screws to fit above, brass, countersunk

$\frac{3}{4}$in brass pins or 3in of $\frac{1}{16}$in brass rod

---

$\frac{1}{16}$in birch plywood or similar, $6\frac{1}{2}$ × 10in for templates

This delightful oval box was not designed with any particular function in mind. It was inspired, in part at least, by the style of traditional hatboxes, and it could be used to store small perfume or pill bottles or essential oils.

The initial oval template can be made in a number of ways. It can be derived from something you already own, such as a small mirror or box, or it can be traced from something similar. Artists' materials and art supply stores stock elliptical templates in a wide variety of sizes.

If you want to work from basics, draw one-quarter of the shape using a French curve of the kind usually available from any office supply store, and duplicate it for the four curved segments which make up the body of the box.

The construction is very simple, although the making process takes patience. The four sides or segments that make up the main box need to be cut to size very accurately. They are then butt-glued to the assembled dividers. The box derives strength from the base, which is glued and screwed on.

The fine $\frac{3}{64}$in wide black/white/black inlay used in the lid decoration is available from guitar and lute makers' suppliers and is useful for a wide variety of fine woodworking applications.

CUTTING LIST

SIDES (figured maple 1 piece)
$3 \times 3 \times 10$in

LID AND BASE (figured maple 4 pieces)
$3\frac{3}{16} \times \frac{5}{16} \times 10$in

LONG DIVIDER (birch plywood 1 piece)
*$2\frac{3}{4} \times \frac{1}{8} \times$ *$8\frac{1}{2}$in

SHORT DIVIDER (birch plywood 1 piece)
*$2\frac{3}{4} \times \frac{1}{8} \times$ *$5\frac{1}{4}$in

Sides cut from $3 \times 3 \times 10$in length

*Allowance for waste

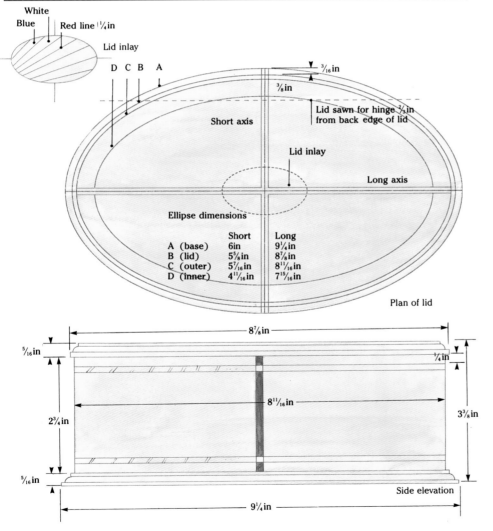

White
Blue
Red line $1\frac{1}{4}$in
Lid inlay

D C B A

$\frac{3}{16}$in
$\frac{3}{8}$in

Short axis

Lid sawn for hinge $\frac{2}{3}$in from back edge of lid

Lid inlay

Long axis

Ellipse dimensions

	Short	Long
A (base)	6in	$9\frac{1}{4}$in
B (lid)	$5\frac{5}{8}$in	$8\frac{7}{8}$in
C (outer)	$5\frac{7}{16}$in	$8\frac{11}{16}$in
D (inner)	$4\frac{11}{16}$in	$7\frac{15}{16}$in

Plan of lid

$8\frac{7}{8}$in
$\frac{5}{16}$in
$\frac{1}{4}$in
$8\frac{11}{16}$in
$2\frac{3}{4}$in
$3\frac{3}{8}$in
$\frac{5}{16}$in
Side elevation
$9\frac{1}{4}$in

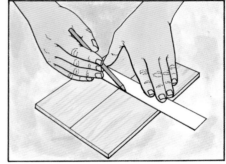

1 First prepare the wood for the lid and base (see pages 16-21), joint the pieces for the base and lid, and plane and sand them even, marking the lines dividing the length and width as shown on the plan.

MAKING THE TEMPLATES

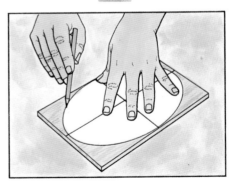

2 Make an oval template from $\frac{1}{16}$in birch plywood, clearly marking the long and short axes. Mark around this on the pieces for the base. Set a marking gauge to $\frac{3}{16}$in and mark around the template, reducing it to this size. Mark around this onto the lid piece.

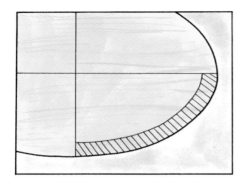

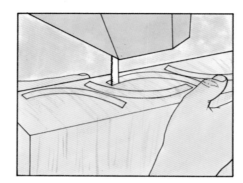

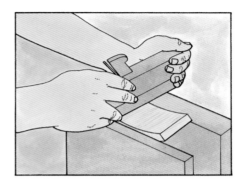

3 Set the marking gauge to $\frac{3}{32}$ in. Mark around the template again and reduce it to this size. Set the marking gauge to $\frac{3}{8}$ in and mark around one-quarter of the remaining template. Cut out this section. Remove $\frac{1}{16}$ in from each end of this piece.

4 Mark out the four pieces for the "sides" or segments forming the body using the template and cut them out on the bandsaw. This will be quite a deep cut for most small workshop bandsaws, so work slowly to give the blade time to clear the waste.

5 Smooth the inside faces of these pieces using a hollow plane, curved scraper, and sandpaper. Hollow planes may be difficult to come by, but with patience you can achieve the same result with a carving gouge. Coat the inside faces with thinned sanding sealer.

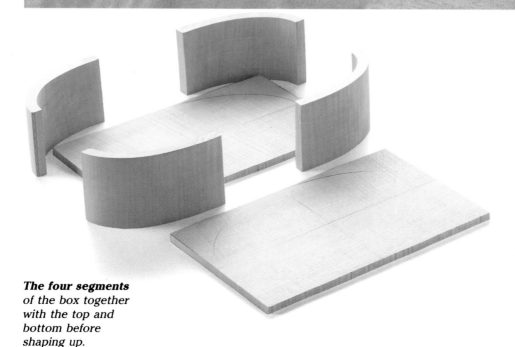

The four segments *of the box together with the top and bottom before shaping up.*

MAKING THE DIVIDERS

6 Veneer the pieces of $\frac{1}{8}$ in birch plywood on both sides with the blue-dyed veneer. When they are dry, trim the pieces square to $8\frac{1}{2} \times 2\frac{3}{4}$ in or $5 \times 2\frac{3}{4}$ in.

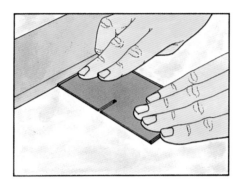

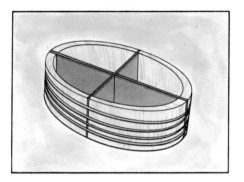

7 Edge-band each piece on one long and both short sides with strips of ebony $\frac{1}{8} \times \frac{3}{16}$in cut from the prepared piece. When dry, plane these bandings flush and lightly sand, taking care not to get ebony dust on the blue veneer.

8 Cut $\frac{5}{32}$in slots halfway along each of the pieces, one from the top (edge-banded edge) and one from the bottom. Make each slightly more than half the width. Seal and sand. Install with the ebony edge banding uppermost.

9 Sand the inside faces of the four side segments smooth and wax them. This is best done now while they are easy to get at (pages 120-121). Set up the pieces as shown in the plan and hold them together with strong rubber bands.

INSTALLING THE INLAY

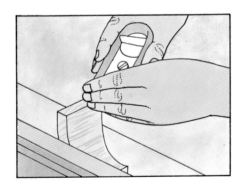

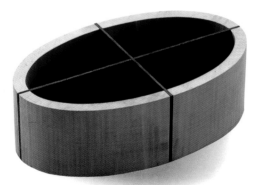

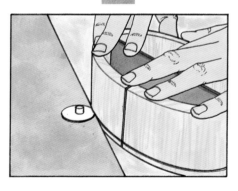

10 If the pieces have been accurately cut, the joints should fit snugly. Carefully plane anything that is not perfectly square. Then take apart and repeat the whole operation with glue. When dry, plane and sand the outer surfaces flat and even.

The assembled box with the dividers showing through the sides to give dramatic visual effect.

11 Cut a groove for the decorative inlay strips with a $\frac{1}{8}$in slot cutter as shown. Glue the strips in place, making sure they are the correct length. When dry, scrape flush, then sand and seal.

SHAPING LID AND BASE

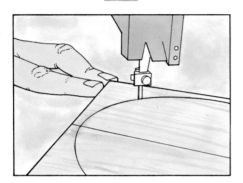

12 Carefully cut the lid and base to shape on the bandsaw and smooth them exactly to size. The disk sander is an excellent tool to use for doing this.

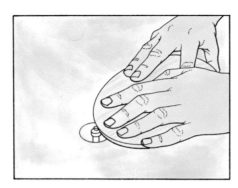

13 Form a curve around the top edge of the base and lid using a ⅛in corner-round bit with guide pin/bearing. Do this with at least three cuts, increasing the height of the bit each time. The final cut must remove only the smallest amount of material. This prevents scorching.

MAKING THE LID INLAY

14 Make a template in 1/16in birch plywood, 2in long, tapering from ¼in to ⅛in. Cut around this to produce four pieces each of blue and white veneer. Also cut seven strips of red veneer 1/16in wide and 2in long.

15 Tape waxed paper to a small, flat board and secure one tapered piece along one edge by taping its extreme ends. Brush a little 15 percent diluted white glue along its edge, place a strip of red *edge up* next to it, brush on a little glue and repeat, taping each piece.

16 Cover with a piece of paper, some carpet underlay, and another small board, then clamp up. Repeat with the other tapered pieces and join the two halves in the same way. When dry, cut out your oval using the prepared brass template.

INSTALLING THE LID INLAY

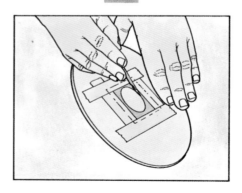

17 Tape the oval template to the lid, making sure you line up the long and short axes. Cut around the inside of the template with a craft knife, angling the blade slightly to produce a slightly smaller oval. Remove the wood in this area to a depth of 1/64in.

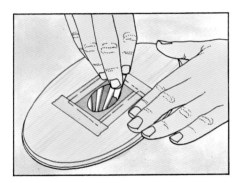

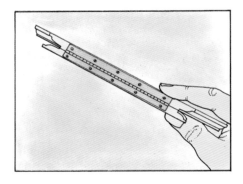

18 Glue the oval motif into this recess, sanding as necessary; it does not need to fit perfectly. When it is dry, tape the template in position again and work around the inside edge with the prepared scraper, to produce a neat groove for the black/white/black inlay.

19 Dip the inlay in hot water for a few seconds to make it more flexible, and then secure it around a block the size of the required oval. When it is dry and has taken on the required shape, it can be glued into the groove. When dry, trim to length, glue and scrape flush.

20 Using a bandsaw and fence, cut the lid into two, ⁹⁄₁₆in from the back edge, by taping it to a board with its edge parallel to the lid's long axis. Prepare a piece of fine piano hinge and fit with an incomplete rabbet on the back edge of the lid, half the thickness of the closed hinge.

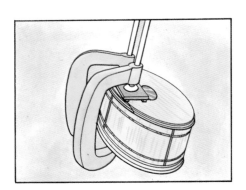

21 Smooth and wax all external surfaces, and glue and screw in the base. Glue the back edge of the lid. Pin using four ³⁄₄in brass pins (cut off heads) or pieces of ¹⁄₁₆in brass rod. Space rods to enter between the hinge screws.

The finished box – the corner-round molding on the lid and base gives a pleasing decorative finish.

JEWELRY BOX IN BURL VENEER

The beautiful curves of this unusual and striking jewelry box are complemented perfectly by the rich and luxuriously figured book-matched American burl walnut.

By careful selection from four consecutive sheets of veneer including some lighter sapwood, it is possible to create the effect of a dark figure "draped" symmetrically over a lighter colored box. The decorative stringing and boxwood edgings clearly delineate the elegant shape, and the exterior is French-polished. This is a complex project, and considerable care and planning are required. You will need to make three templates and three forms, two forms for constructing and veneering the lid and one for veneering the sides. A hollow plane, so-called from the cut it makes and not from the shape of the sole, is an important tool for making these and for shaping the sides.

Plan of tray

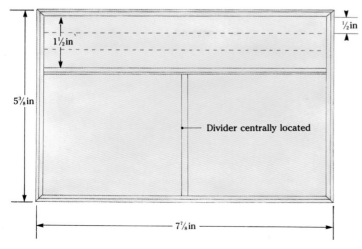

$\frac{1}{2}$in

$1\frac{1}{2}$in

$5\frac{3}{8}$in

Divider centrally located

$7\frac{7}{8}$in

Ring run cross-section

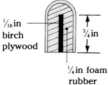

Velvet

$\frac{1}{16}$in birch plywood

$\frac{3}{4}$in

$\frac{1}{4}$in foam rubber

VENEERS

INNER EDGES (2 identical pieces each)
4¾ × 2in

INNER EDGES (2 identical pieces each)
6¾ × 1in

FRONT (2 identical pieces each)
5 × 3¾in

BACK (2 identical pieces each)
5 × 3¾in

SIDES (2 identical pieces each)
7½ × 4¼in

LID (4 identical pieces each)
4¾ × 3½in

TOOLKIT

For basic kit, see pages 8-13

½in straight bit • ¹⁄₁₆in slot bit • No. 14 hollow plane (see introduction, far left) • Curved scrapers • Sanding drum • Veneer press or boards, clamps and cauls • Round, flat, and triangular needle files • Fine beading scraper (made from piece of hacksaw blade) • Purfling cutter (available from musical instrument makers' suppliers) • 45 degree block • Rubber bands

MATERIALS

A pair of small brass quadrant hinges

A small, good-quality brass box lock

Mother-of-pearl or similar for escutcheon

Fine brass pins, ½in long

Fine white/black/white stringing, 7ft

Decorative banding of your choice, 5ft

Fine ³⁄₆₄in black/white/black inlay , 3½in
(see introduction, page 76)

⅛in square boxwood line, 7ft

Fabric, blue moire or similar, 32 × 6in

Velvet, to match above, 24 × 9in

Thin poster board 33 × 9in

Masonite, ⅛in 2 pieces 1¾ × 5½in

Low-density foam rubber, ¼in thick,
8 × 8in

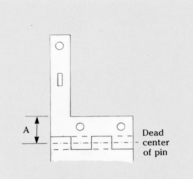

The thickness of the veneered sides where the lid meets the box will depend on your hinges. It should be exactly the same as the distance from the *center* of the pin (A) to the edge of the main flap.

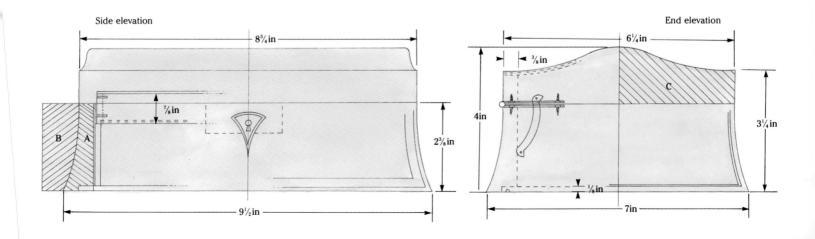

PREPARING THE LID

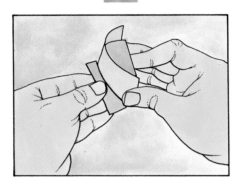

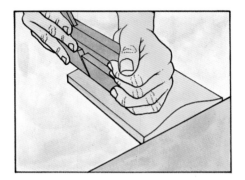

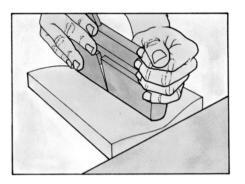

1 Use $\frac{1}{16}$ in birch plywood to make three templates (see plans). These are shown by the crosshatched areas marked A, B, and C and are for the curved sides and lid. See plans for note on thickness of sides.

2 Take a piece of scrap wood measuring $5\frac{1}{4} \times 9 \times 1\frac{1}{4}$ in. Mark the profile of the lid as high as possible on each end and remove the waste *above* the line with a hollow plane. Smooth with a curved scraper and sandpaper on a curved sanding block.

3 In the same way make a piece $6\frac{1}{2} \times 9\frac{1}{4} \times 1$ in, mark the lid profile at each end as *low* as it will fit, and remove the waste below the lines and smooth as before. The two forms should fit neatly together.

MAKING THE SIDES

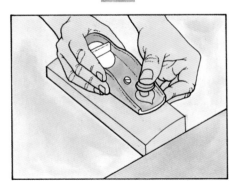

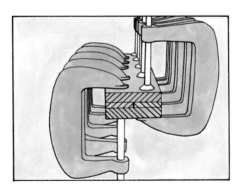

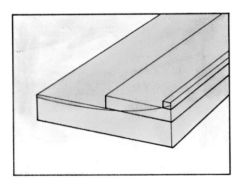

4 Take another piece of scrap wood, $10\frac{3}{4} \times 2\frac{2}{3} \times \frac{3}{4}$ in and mark the profile of the sides on each end. Remove the waste *inside* the lines to produce a convex form that will fit neatly into the shape of the sides. Smooth as before.

5 Glue the $\frac{1}{2}$ in and $\frac{1}{4}$ in pieces of MDF in pairs as shown, front and back together followed by the two sides. Glue a piece of scrap hardwood, $\frac{5}{32}$ in square, along the bottom outside edge to complete the stepped pieces.

6 Using the template, draw the profile for the sides on the end of each of these pieces, and use a hollow plane to remove the waste down to these lines. The profile does not need to be exact at this stage; finer shaping is done later when the box has been assembled.

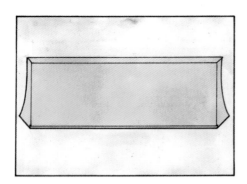

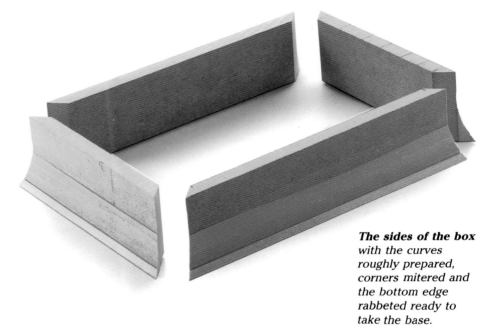

7 Now the pieces must be mitered. This can be done with a miter saw, a miter trimmer, or a small block plane, checking the 45-degrees with a sliding bevel. When you are satisfied, cut a rabbet $\frac{9}{64}$in deep and $\frac{3}{8}$in wide along the inside bottom edges.

*The **sides of the box** with the curves roughly prepared, corners mitered and the bottom edge rabbeted ready to take the base.*

ASSEMBLY

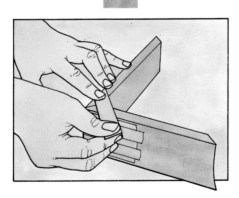

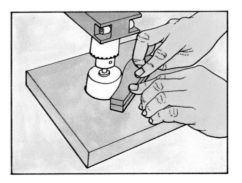

8 Tape the pieces together to check for fit and squareness and number them. Glue the pieces together in pairs, holding them with masking tape around the outside of the joint and across the top and bottom of the corner. When both halves are dry, glue them together.

9 Cut slots on the *inside* of each corner, using a slot cutter set to cut at a height of $\frac{3}{8}$in. Glue a $1\frac{3}{8}$in circle of $\frac{1}{16}$in birch plywood into each corner with the grain of the face veneer running *across* the corner. Trim when dry.

10 Now join the two prepared pieces of hardwood for the lid sides face to face with double-sided tape, and mark the lid profile on one face. Cut out the two pieces as one and remove the saw marks with a sanding drum mounted in a drill stand.

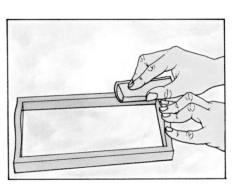

11 Measure the inside dimensions of the box and miter the corners of the lid components to produce a frame the same size. Glue and tape these pieces together. Sand the joints level with a curved sanding block.

The main framework of the box and the curved lid frame before the plywood top is added.

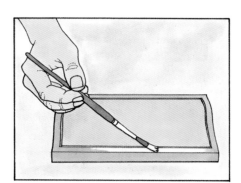

12 Place the lid frame, with the lower lid form inside, on a setting-up board, and use paper shims to make sure it is flush with the lid frame. Spread glue around the top edge of the frame and place the birch plywood, a piece of carpet underlay, and the upper lid form in place.

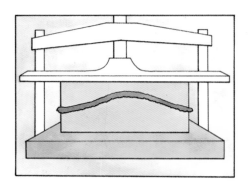

13 Clamp firmly or put in a veneer press. Repeat the previous step for the second piece of plywood, gluing the whole surface of the plywood to guarantee complete adhesion. This will bring the thickness to $\frac{1}{8}$ in, producing an extremely rigid and lightweight lid.

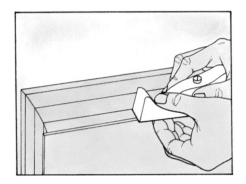

14 When the glue is dry, remove the form, tape the box together from inside, mark the front and back, and place in a vice with the front facing upward. Plane off the excess plywood from the front edge of the lid.

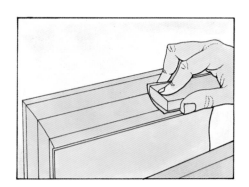

15 Use a hollow plane, then a curved scraper, and finally a curved sanding block, to reduce the front to a single, smooth curve, checking the profile with template B. Be sure to keep the edge of the lid at right angles to the base. Repeat for the back and sides.

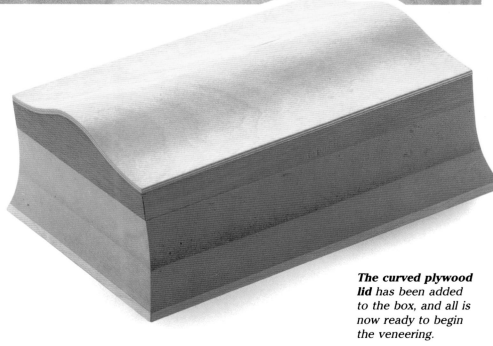

The curved plywood lid has been added to the box, and all is now ready to begin the veneering.

VENEERING THE BOX

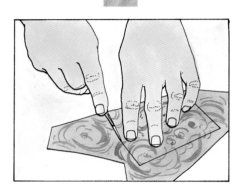

16 Cut out and flatten the pieces of veneer itemized in the cutting list. Take great care when using the craft knife (see pages 45-46, steps 3-5). Leave until completely flat and dry.

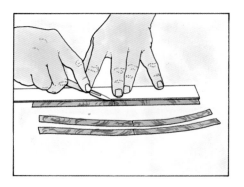

17 Book-match the two $4\frac{3}{4} \times 2$ in pieces to produce a piece $9\frac{1}{2} \times 2$ in (see pages 45-46). When dry, cut four strips, each $9\frac{1}{2} \times \frac{1}{2}$ in from the prepared piece and four more strips $6\frac{3}{4} \times \frac{1}{2}$ in, two each from the two $6\frac{3}{4} \times 1$ in pieces.

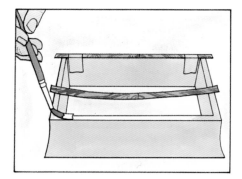

18 Veneer one of the long book-matched strips, one along the front and one along the back inside edges of the box, making sure that the joints are exactly at the middle points. Do both together and clamp.

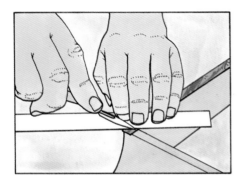

19 When dry, carefully trim the outside edges flush with the outside of the box and miter the corners. Take two identical prepared strips, $6\frac{3}{4} \times \frac{1}{2}$in, miter these and veneer them in place, applying pressure as before. Repeat for the lid.

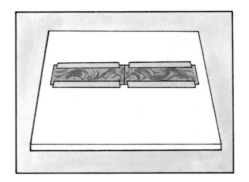

20 Book-match two of the identical $5 \times 3\frac{3}{4}$in pieces, to produce a piece $10 \times 3\frac{3}{4}$in When dry, cut a strip 1in wide from the top and set aside under a weighted board.

21 Veneer the main piece to the front of the box using the prepared form, carpet underlay, and clamps. Make sure that the join is exactly central. Overlap the top edge as little as possible – around $\frac{1}{64}$in. Veneer the 1in strip to the front edge of the lid.

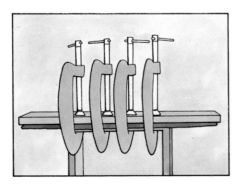

22 Take the other two $5 \times 3\frac{3}{4}$in pieces, book-match, and repeat for the back of the box. Veneer the sides in the same way (these are not book-matched), cutting strips $1\frac{5}{8}$in wide from the top of each and veneering to the lid ends (as illustrated).

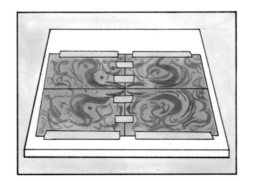

23 Join two long sides of two of the $4\frac{3}{4} \times 3\frac{1}{2}$in pieces and repeat with the other two pieces. Now join these two pieces to produce one four-way book-matched piece $9\frac{1}{4} \times 7$in.

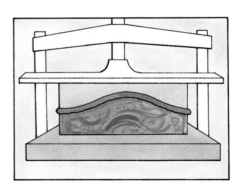

24 Set up the lid on a board with the lower form inside it. Apply glue to the lid, then the veneer, making sure it is perfectly symmetrical, and then the upper lid form. Place in a press or clamp. When dry, trim the overlapping veneer from edges of box and lid.

INLAYING STRINGING

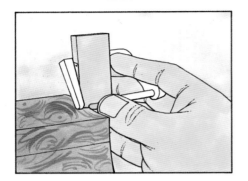

| 25 | Reunite box and lid. Use a purfling cutter to cut the front and top of the lid to the width of the chosen stringing plus the boxwood square less $\frac{1}{32}$ in. The cutter here was improvised using scrap wood, a craft knife and a C-clamp. |

| 26 | Now make a cut in from the edge of the sides and back to suit your white/black/white stringing and boxwood edge banding, as before. Carefully reinforce all these cuts with a craft knife and remove the veneer from all edges with a sharp $\frac{1}{4}$ in chisel. |

The veneer has been trimmed away from the edges, ready for the addition of the decorative stringing.

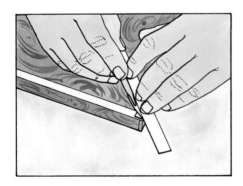

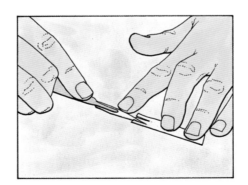

| 27 | Separate the lid and box, then glue a piece of the decorative stringing to the top edge of one end of the lid. Tape it securely in place. Repeat at the other end. Use a craft knife to miter the ends of each piece, and glue and tape the mitered pieces in place for the front and back. |

| 28 | Repeat for all edges of the front. The pieces to go down the curved front sides will need to be dipped in hot water and partly disassembled. Now similarly fit the fine white/black/white lines all round both ends and back. |

| 29 | Cut out the waste along all external edges to take the boxwood edge banding. Soak a piece of boxwood, $6\frac{3}{4}$ in long, in hot water for about half a minute, and glue and tape this piece in place along one curved side edge of the lid. Repeat at the other end. |

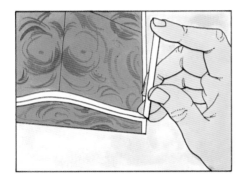

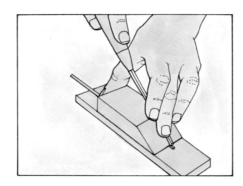

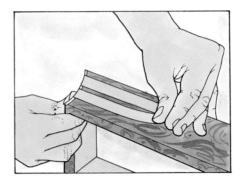

30 When dry, carefully cut a two-way miter – vertical and horizontal – at each end of each of the pieces. Use a ¼in chisel to make initial shallow 45-degree cuts, removing the waste with fine, splitting cuts, along the grain from the ends of the pieces.

31 Fit a piece of the boxwood along the front edge of the lid, using a 45-degree block and a ¼in chisel to miter the ends. Do horizontal miters first, then the vertical. Repeat for the back of lid. Fit the short, vertical pieces at each corner of the lid, cutting two-way miters.

32 Glue and tape pieces of soaked boxwood at each corner while still pliable. When dry, trim flush and cut a two-way miter at the corners (see step 30). Note the angle of the vertical miter is less than 45 degrees.

33 Fit the four bottom pieces in place and, when dry, reunite the box and lid and trim all stringing and edge banding down to veneer level by first chiseling, then scraping with a curved scraper, and finally sanding. Cut the base to size, drill and screw in place.

The box and lid together with the stringing and edge banding trimmed carefully back to the level of the veneer.

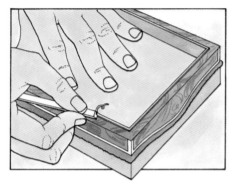

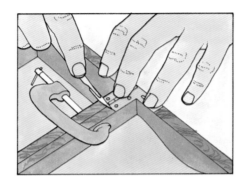

34 Separate the box and lid. Make a cut around the inside edge of the box with purfling cutter set to suit your white/black/white stringing, but do not allow the extra $\frac{1}{32}$ in. Reinforce this cut; remove the veneer. Glue and tape in place, mitering the corners. When dry, level and sand.

35 Repeat step 34 for the lid. Then fit the hinges and lock as in pages 72-74. This is a very delicate procedure which can make or break the final result, so take time and care, and be sure to get it right.

36 Transfer the shape of the escutcheon onto a piece of mother-of-pearl and carefully cut out using a jeweler's piercing saw. Bring the edges exactly to shape using 240-grit garnet paper on a curved block.

TRAY CONSTRUCTION

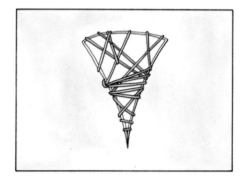

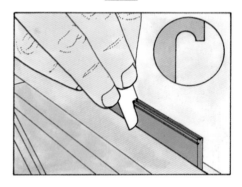

37 Glue a slightly overlength piece of fine black/white/black fiber stringing to each long side, holding it in place with thread. Cut a very acute angle at the bottom end of these pieces to form a neat joint there. Do this with a chisel, held almost flat.

38 Use a craft knife to trim the top of the side pieces, forming a miter that bisects the angle formed between the long side and the beginning of the top edge. Glue and tape the top piece in place. When dry, sand the back of the escutcheon, inlay, and cut the keyhole.

39 Use a small beading scraper (profile shown above) to form a bead along the top outside edge of the pieces for the front, back, sides, and long divider. This is done by scraping alternately on the outer and upper edges, holding the wood vertically and flat.

40 Measure box interior and make both tray dimensions $\frac{1}{8}$in smaller. Miter the corners of each piece and cut the grooves along the bottom inside edges using the $\frac{5}{64}$in bit to take the base. Cut the base to size and stick moire to the underside and glue.

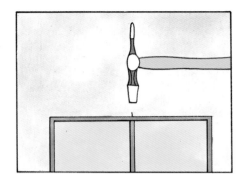

41 When it is dry, cut the long divider exactly to length and glue in place, with the bead to the front. Then position the short, front divider. Drill and hammer in two brass pins at each of the points where the dividers meet the outside edges, cut off the heads and smooth.

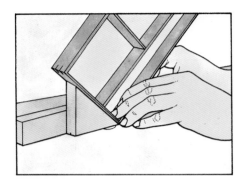

42 Make white/black/white veneers, $\frac{3}{8} \times 3\frac{1}{2}$in, with all the grain lengthwise. Glue and clamp. Using a spline jig (see page 51, step 30), cut $\frac{1}{16}$in slots, $\frac{1}{4}$in long and $\frac{3}{16}$in from the top and bottom of each corner.

LINING THE BOX

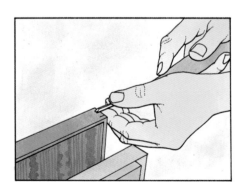

43 When the sandwich is dry, plane each long edge flat, and cut triangular pieces a little over-size. Glue them in place into the slots, with the grain running across the corners. Allow to dry, then chisel off the excess, working in from each corner. Sand smooth.

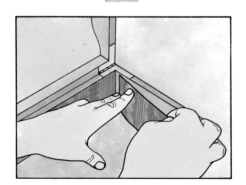

44 Line the box as shown on pages 74-75, cutting around the lid template to shape the poster board for inside the ends of the lid. The bottom of the box and inside the top of the lid are lined with velvet. Cut the poster board $\frac{5}{64}$in under-size for these areas.

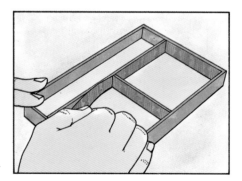

45 Line front tray compartments thus: side/front, back/divider, and bottom (velvet). Make the pieces for the side/front before you measure for the back/divider. Finally, with the pieces so far in place, measure for the bottom velvet piece and cut it $\frac{5}{64}$in smaller.

MAKING THE BACKGROUND

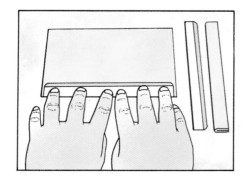

46 Cut three strips of birch plywood ⅛in less than the internal length of the tray. Round over the top edges and cover with ¼in foam held with double-sided tape as shown in the plan.

47 Cut a piece of velvet 6in wide and ¾in longer than the plywood and spray the wrong side of this and the three prepared pieces of birch plywood with adhesive. Cover the three pieces with the velvet as shown in the plan.

48 Finish the ends by using a craft knife to make horizontal cuts in line with the top of the plywood. Fold in the two side flaps, gluing and then folding down the top piece, and gluing it in place, too. If these fit snugly in the trays, it should not be necessary to glue them in place.

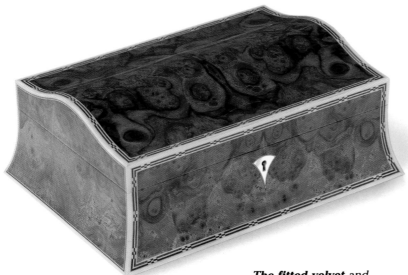

The fitted velvet and moire-lined interior of the finished box completes this very individual gift.

DECORATIVE TECHNIQUES

The use of inlays, bandings, and decorative techniques will personalize your work and make each box stunningly individual. Let your imagination be free to take advantage of these new techniques to raise your work to the advanced stages of craftsmanship, where the real joy of box-making can find its own reward.

VENEERCRAFT

Veneercraft is really a simple form of marquetry, and as such it is a good introduction to that art. The difference is that in veneercraft you do not cut the subject matter into the background. The picture is made by overlaying the elements rather than by fitting them into shapes that have been cut with a craft knife.

Draw your own design and experiment! Quite often, veneercraft is used on work that might be found in a child's room. Because it stands proud of the backing material, it adds a tactile dimension, which children enjoy.

TOOLKIT AND MATERIALS

For basic kit, see pages 8-13	Tracing paper
Cutting board	White glue (diluted)
Veneer press or clamps and cauls	Veneers of your choice

*A **quirky piece** of veneercraft, ideal for applying to a "fun" box.*

1 Carefully draw the design of your choice and then trace it on a piece of good-quality tracing paper. When you are using this technique, it is preferable that the design is not too intricate.

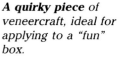

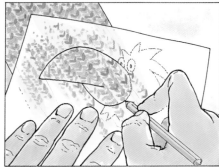

2 Trace the shape of the bill onto a piece of veneer of your choice and carefully cut it out using a craft knife. The design can be traced fairly boldly because detail is not really critical with this technique.

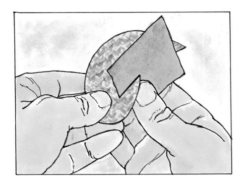

3 Cut out the line for the "mouth" and enlarge it with sandpaper to take a thin sliver of black veneer. Glue this in place and trim it flush when the glue is dry.

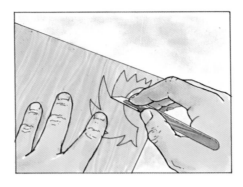

4 Trace the shape of the bird's head onto your chosen veneer and carefully cut it out. Trim the joint between the two shapes so that they fit really well.

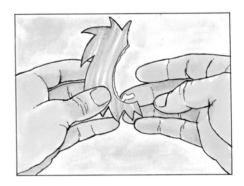

5 When you are satisfied with the fit of the parts, apply glue to one piece and tape them together, making sure that they are flush and fitting snugly.

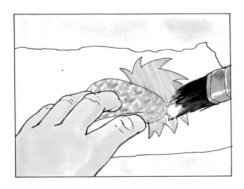

6 Now apply 10 percent diluted white glue to the back of the assembled head and glue this to your chosen ground. Put it in a veneer press or clamp it firmly. When the complete assembly is dry, sand off the raised edges a little.

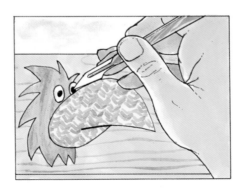

7 Now glue in place the whites of the eyes and then the pupils. All sorts of different expressions can be achieved at this stage, so it is worth experimenting a little.

8 Allow the glue to dry, then sand the eyes lightly, being careful not to get black dust into the whites. Finish with a coat of sanding sealer if desired (see pages 120-121).

MAKING COLORED LINES

The inlaid line, which is used to border a panel or just to add interest to a plain wooden lid, is the simplest of all inlaid decorations. In its basic form it is just a single, thin line of a contrasting wood. Boxwood is usually preferred in a dark wood, while ebony is often used in a light wood for maximum contrast.

In the sequence overleaf, this is taken one stage further. A sandwich of various colored veneers is made up; strips are then cut off on the bandsaw and inlaid as you would inlay a solid line.

It is usually a good idea to have a thin black line on each side of the colored "core," but if you are working with dark woods, you might like to reverse this and have an outer line of boxwood or chestnut.

This is a very easy technique, which is made even easier if you have a small veneer press. The possibilities are endless, but don't get carried away. Think about the combination of colors and design that you actually want for the piece you are working on.

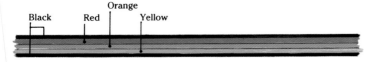

Black   Red   Orange   Yellow

A simple colored line is easy to make, yet it can bring to the most ordinary of boxes an unexpected degree of sophistication.

TOOLKIT AND MATERIALS

For basic kit, see pages 8-13

Setting-up board

Masking tape

White glue (diluted)

Carpet underlay

Veneer press or clamps and cauls

Veneers of your choice: boxwood is usually preferred in a dark wood, and ebony in a light wood

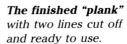

The finished "plank" with two lines cut off and ready to use.

The colored line applied to a panel.

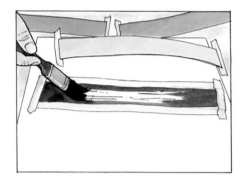

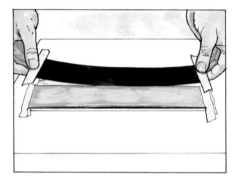

1 Cut the pieces of veneer to the required size. This is best done by cutting around a template made from scrap wood. Stick a piece of ½in masking tape, 3¼in long, across each end of each piece covering about ¼in.

2 Fix one of the black pieces to the setting-up board with paper underneath. Apply 10 percent diluted white glue evenly and sparingly with a 1in brush. Tape the next color in place and apply glue as before.

3 Repeat until you come to the second black and tape this in position. Place a piece of paper, some carpet underlay, and another board on top and put the whole sandwich in the veneer press or clamp it with cauls.

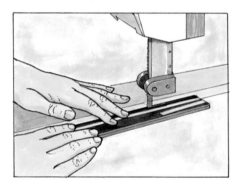

4 When it is dry, cut off the taped ends and plane one edge until it is quite even. You will be producing complete shavings with evidence of all the colors you have used showing on the edge.

5 Now tape a piece of masonite to the prepared piece as shown. This will prevent the bottom layer of black from breaking away when you bandsaw the strips off.

6 Set the bandsaw to cut off strips ¹⁄₃₂in thick and test this on scrap wood first. Bandsaw off as many strips as you need for your job.

MAKING CROSS-BANDING

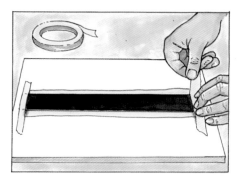

Cross-banded lines have two basic elements: first, an outer layer made up of one or more lines and, second, the "core," which is formed using pieces of well-figured wood with the grain running across at right angles to the rest of the line – hence cross-banding.

With care it is possible in a small workshop to make cross-banded lines that are vastly superior to commercially available ones. These often suffer from "gappy" cross-banding, which is caused by the pieces that make up the core not being properly jointed.

| 1 | Prepare the cocobolo (see pages 16-21). The end will be cut square on the bandsaw. |

Then prepare two black/black/white/black "sandwiches" (see opposite). Tape one piece to the setting-up board with the two blacks at the bottom.

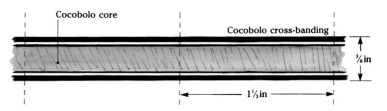

Cocobolo core

Cocobolo cross-banding

⅜ in

1⅓ in

Effective and often dramatic, cross-banding, although easy to do, offers unrivalled opportunities for original decoration.

TOOLKIT AND MATERIALS

For basic kit, see pages 8-13

Setting-up board

Masking tape

White glue (diluted)

Carpet underlay

Veneer press or clamps and cauls

veneers of your choice. The must commonly used are tulipwood, kingwood, and satinwood. In this demonstration cocobolo has been used. Any well-figured wood is suitable depending on the effect you wish to achieve.

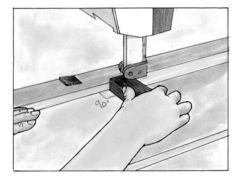

| 2 | Using the bandsaw and a 90-degree guide, cut off eight end grain "slices," ¼ in thick, from |

the prepared piece of cocobolo. Discard the first piece so that the first piece you actually use has two clean, square-cut faces.

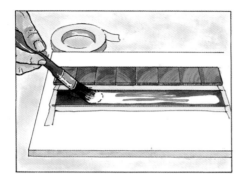

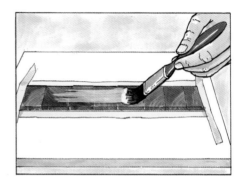

3 Apply 10 percent diluted white glue to the "sandwich" with a brush. A piece of paper placed underneath will stop glue from getting on the board.

4 Line up the cocobolo slices in place, gluing between them. Tape them together and to the board, and wipe off any excess glue. Place a piece of paper, then some carpet underlay, and finally another board on top. Place in the veneer press or clamp with cauls.

5 When the glue is dry, remove the tape. Clean off the top surface of the cocobolo if necessary and glue on the second black/black/white/black "sandwich" as before. Make sure that the double black layer is upward – that is, on the outside of the finished line.

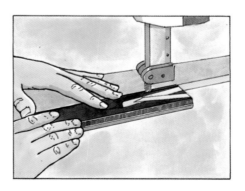

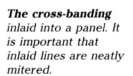

The cross-banding inlaid into a panel. It is important that inlaid lines are neatly mitered.

6 Using a small and very finely set block plane, cut back one edge until it is quite even and the planing produces a complete shaving of the whole edge of the "sandwich."

7 Tape a piece of masonite to the underside (see page 98, step 5). Cut off the strips as required on the bandsaw. A thickness of about $\frac{1}{32}$in is about right for most purposes.

MAKING GEOMETRIC LINES

The final and most complex line dealt with here is similar in format to the cross-banding. Again it has two elements, an outer layer made up of a line or lines, and an inner, decorative "core."

The core in this case is made up from colored veneers, laminated, re-cut, and arranged to form the final pattern.

It is absolutely essential that the veneers used are of an identical thickness. Even a difference of less than $\frac{1}{64}$in is multiplied to almost an $\frac{1}{8}$in when using a thickness of six veneers for the core.

You will need to make a jig to tighten the elements of the core when they are being glued together and to the outer lines. This is formed by joining two pieces of particle board or similar by two pieces of fine "studding," threaded brass or steel rod, and using two wing nuts to exert inward pressure (see plan on this page).

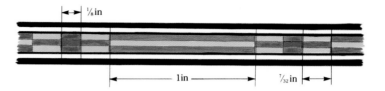

This plan *shows the arrangement of colors and the dimensions for the line featured in the demonstration. Choose colors to suit your own projects.*

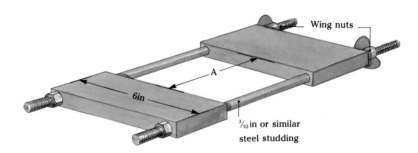

Ensure that the studding *(threaded rod) is long enough to allow the tightening jig to accommodate the full length of the core of your line.*

TOOLKIT AND MATERIALS

For basic kit, see pages 8-13

Graph paper

Setting-up board

Masking tape

White glue (diluted)

Carpet underlay

Veneer press or clamps and cauls

Veneers of your choice

Tightening jig (see plan on this page)

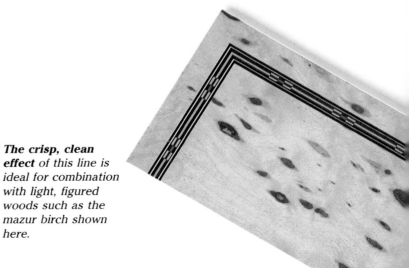

The crisp, clean effect *of this line is ideal for combination with light, figured woods such as the mazur birch shown here.*

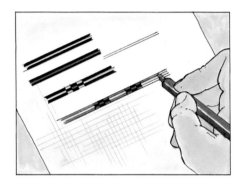

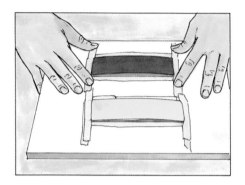

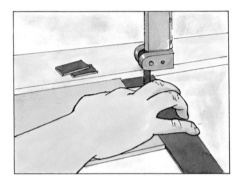

| 1 | First work out carefully exactly what design you want. This is best done on graph paper, filling in the color you want with felt pens. Experiment a little to get the feel of it. |

| 2 | To produce the pattern shown here, first make the following veneer "sandwiches" (see page 98): 2 blue/2 yellow/2 blue: full length; 2 yellow/2 blue/2 yellow: $\frac{1}{2}$ length; 2 blue/2 red/2 blue: $\frac{1}{2}$ length. |

| 3 | Using the bandsaw and a 90-degree guide, cut the following pieces across the grain: 2 blue/2 yellow/2 blue: 8 pieces, 1in long; 2 yellow/2 blue/2 yellow: 14 pieces, $\frac{1}{4}$in long; 2 blue/2 red/2 blue: 7 pieces, $\frac{1}{8}$in long. |

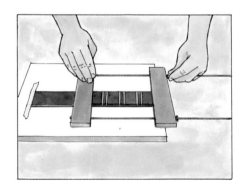

| 4 | Use a craft knife to trim any splintered pieces off the bottom edges caused by the bandsawing. This is a tricky operation, so watch your fingers in the process. |

| 5 | Tape one of the black/black/white/black sandwiches to the setting-up board with the two blacks at the bottom and set the tightening jig (see previous page) to take the first 13 pieces only, starting and finishing with a blue/yellow/blue 1in piece. |

| 6 | Apply 10 percent diluted white glue to the first half of the bottom sandwich; use a 1in brush and apply glue evenly and sparingly. |

7 Put the first 13 pieces in place, gluing their adjacent edges. As in all operations of this kind, care and attention to detail are of the utmost importance for a perfect fit.

8 Put the tightening jig in position and tighten until the pieces just start to pop up. Clean off excess glue, place a piece of scrap wood faced with waxed paper on the pieces as above, and put in the veneer press. Tighten the jig, then apply full pressure in the press.

9 Repeat with the second half, and when it is dry, remove any unevenness from the top surface by light sanding with a block. Work carefully and deliberately without applying too much pressure to the piece.

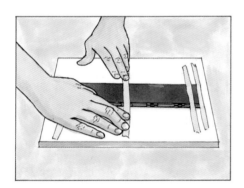

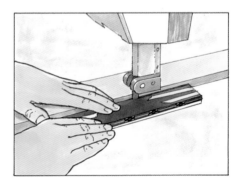

10 Now apply more glue and glue on the second black/black/white/black sandwich as before. Make sure that the double black layer is upward – that is, on the outside of the finished line.

11 Now plane one edge with a sharp and finely set block plane until it is quite even and straight, and until the planing produces complete shavings from the whole of the side.

12 Tape a piece of masonite to the underside (see page 98, step 5) and cut off $1/32$ in strips as required on the bandsaw, keeping the piece pressed tight against the fence throughout the whole operation.

PARQUETRY

Parquetry is the traditional technique of using repeated geometric veneer shapes to produce an overall pattern. Sometimes this is achieved by using different veneers, but more often, as here, the same wood with the grain running in different directions is used. Here you are shown how to produce a classic parquetry design.

Ash is a good wood to use as it has a very visible grain, and the contrast between the two grain directions shows up well. Oak would do equally well, or if you wanted a darker effect, rosewood or any wood with a good streaky figure would be suitable.

Choose your own dimensions, but you will need to make a metal template for cutting the strips. You can use plywood instead, but it is not as good in this application because it is too soft. The easiest solution initially is to use something that you already have: a steel ruler is ideal. This basic technique can be used to produce a wide range of pleasing effects, but give careful thought to planning exactly what you want. Take your time and make readable plans.

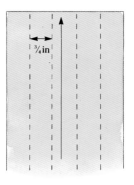

The arrow indicates the direction of the grain; the dotted lines show where the cuts should be made. Work carefully and precisely.

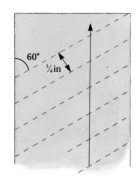

The diagonal cuts, made at an angle of 60 degrees to the grain as indicated by the dotted lines, must be just as precise.

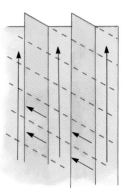

The technique relies for its effect on subtle changes in the direction of the grain. Ash, which was used here, is particularly well suited to the process.

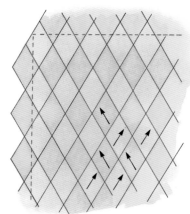

Make a careful plan before you begin, remembering that symmetry is all-important. Use a steel ruler or some other hard, straight edge for cutting.

TOOLKIT AND MATERIALS

For basic kit, see pages 8-13	Waxed paper
Draftsman's plastic triangle square	Carpet underlay
Veneer press or clamps and cauls	Masking tape
	White glue (diluted)
Veneers of your choice	

PREPARING THE STRIPS

1 Cut five strips of ash, each $\frac{3}{4}$in wide by 6in long, along the grain. It is best to use a metal template; a 6in steel ruler was used here. Some fine sandpaper stuck to the reverse side of the ruler will stop it from slipping while you make the cuts.

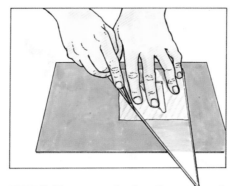

2 Now cut a further five strips of the same dimensions, but at an angle of 60 degrees to the grain. This is best done making the first cut using a draftsman's plastic triangle square and subsequent cuts using the steel ruler or template.

FORMING THE PANEL

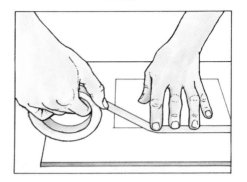

3 Tape a piece of waxed paper $5\frac{3}{4}\times8$in to a setting-up board. If you are working to different dimensions, the waxed paper should be about $\frac{3}{8}$in smaller in length and width than all your strips laid out next to one another.

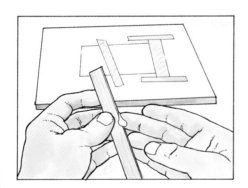

4 Place one cross-grain strip down the right-hand edge of the waxed paper panel, taping both ends securely in place. Apply a little glue to the edge of a straight-grain piece and tape this in place. Sometimes a little tape halfway along the length is helpful.

5 Repeat, alternating cross- and straight-grained strips, until you have five strips in place. Cover with paper, a piece of carpet underlay, and another board, and place in a veneer press or clamp with cauls. Stop halfway so that the strips already glued don't dry too much.

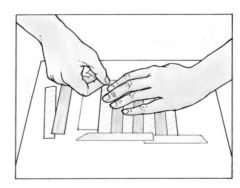

6 When this is dry, remove the pieces from the press, glue the other five pieces in place, and return to the press in exactly the same manner as before.

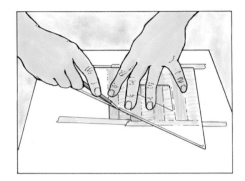

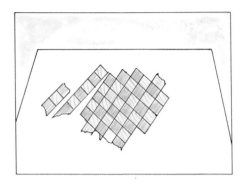

7 Remove from the press and cut the glued-up sheet into ³⁄₄in strips using the the draftsman's square for the first cut and then the template at an angle of 60 degrees to the joints. These pieces will vary in length.

8 Join these new strips as before, but with the longest pieces diagonally across your paper panel. The shorter pieces can be used to fill in the corners.

9 Juggle the pieces a bit before you commit yourself. Again, it is safer to glue these strips in two batches. Remove from the press when dry and take off the tape.

SETTING IN THE PANEL

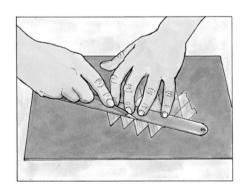

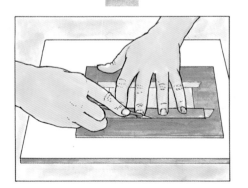

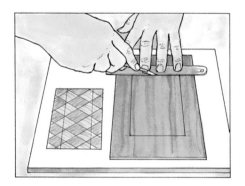

10 Trim the edges of the assembled piece to produce a panel of your required dimensions. Do this with a craft knife and steel ruler.

11 Tape your prepared panel to the piece to be decorated. Here, a padauk-veneered panel is used. Make sure that it is in exactly the right position. Tape the long sides first, running off each end but not overlapping the long sides. Cut along both edges.

12 Tape along the short sides and cut these lines. Remove the panel and reinforce these lines with the craft knife and steel ruler. Place the ruler on the *outside* of the rectangle so that the area is not slightly enlarged by the blade.

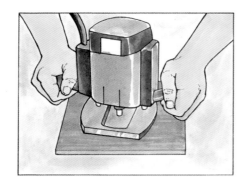

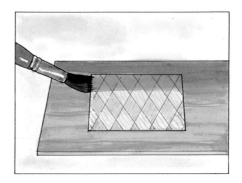

13 Remove the veneer from inside these cuts, either carefully by hand, or by freehand routing using a wide, straight bit with bottom cut. Cut the edges and corners by hand after the main bulk has been removed.

14 Glue and tape the panel in position, making sure that it is the same way around as originally intended. Place in the veneer press or clamp with cauls. When dry, scrape the surface absolutely level with a cabinet scraper, bearing in mind grain direction.

15 Now the panel is ready for finishing. If you have used padauk, be careful because its color runs very easily, and you must protect a light panel by keeping the finishing of the two areas separate initially. Seal the color, then finish (see pages 114-123).

The finished panel, waxed and polished, simple but effective.

MARQUETRY

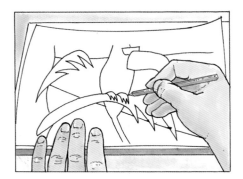

Marquetry is the name given to the art of producing recognizable pictures using the distinctive colors and grain patterns of different veneers. There are many different ways of producing a marquetry picture – the "window" method, demonstrated here, is just one of them. Make a tracing of your picture, reverse it, and tape the top edge to a flat cutting board. In the "window" method, the background is made by tracing through the essential elements onto the veneer and joining them to produce a complete panel into which the other elements are cut. The remaining elements are set into the background. The whole operation is done in reverse because when you cut the windows, and then the pieces to fit into them, the way the blade cuts into the veneer produces a tighter fit at the bottom of the cut because the blade is tapered. This means that you will have much cleaner, tighter joints on the underneath of the picture.

| **1** | Draw the design or your version of it, or draw a completely different design if you prefer, and trace this on good-quality tracing paper. If you are new to the technique, try to keep the design fairly simple. |

TOOLKIT AND MATERIALS

For basic kit, see pages 8-13

Veneer press or clamps and cauls

Tracing paper

Masking tape

White glue (diluted)

Veneers of your choice

Colorful and attractive, marquetry has a naïve yet unquestionable charm.

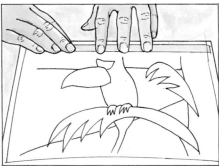

| **2** | Reverse the tracing and tape the top edge to the top of a cutting board. Remember that the operation is carried out in reverse, with the elements being set into the background. You will also need to be able to lift the tracing paper, so secure it along the top edge only. |

MAKING THE BACKGROUND

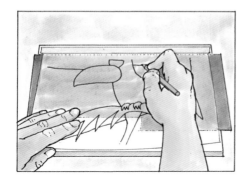

3 Place a piece of light blue veneer, large enough for the sky, under the tracing and trace through the skyline onto it. In this particular picture this is a fairly narrow strip.

4 Cut this line by hand with a craft knife, keeping the angle of cut low. The line does not need to be perfectly straight and should have a natural look.

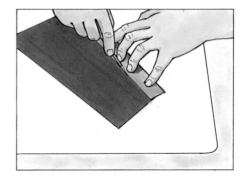

5 Now place this over a piece of dark blue veneer, large enough for the sea, and cut along the edge, taking care to hold the blade firmly against the edge of the sky.

6 Check the fit and rub glue along the edge of one piece and tape them together. Tape "stitches" to pull them together on both sides and pieces along the length where necessary. Rub the joint with the handle of a craft knife or similar to guarantee that it is flush.

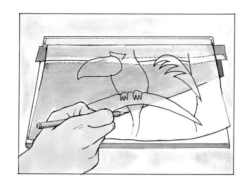

7 Place the sky/sea assembly back under the tracing paper and trace the "shoreline" through. Work in the same manner as before and again not too formally — aim to give it a natural feel.

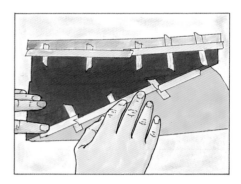

8 Cut this line and place a piece of yellow veneer for the sand under it. Hold this firmly in place, cut along the line, and join as before with glue and tape.

Fitting the features

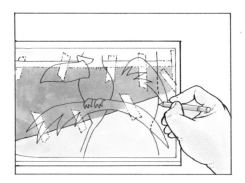

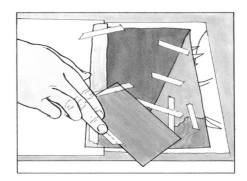

9 When dry, trim the edges square but leave the whole slightly over-size. Tape the top edge of the assembled background in place between the tracing and the cutting board. Both the tracing and the background must be able to be folded up and down easily.

10 As the palm trunk does not fit into a "window," it is treated as part of the background. Trace its profile onto the background – follow the dotted lines shown above. Cut out and cut a piece from your chosen veneer to fit. Glue and tape in position as before to complete the background.

11 Trace the top small branch on the background and carefully cut out this shape, using a fresh knife blade. Tape a piece of green veneer to the underneath, "right," side to cover this "window."

Fitting the beak

The beak is prepared in a slightly different way, in that it is made up complete with its colored stripes before the window is cut for it. This makes the fitting much easier.

12 Now cut through the window slowly and carefully until you have cut all the way around. Remove the piece of veneer and carefully complete any cuts that have not gone right through.

13 Test the piece in place by pushing through from behind. Apply glue to the edges and push it into place, tape, and rub the edges. Repeat steps 11 and 12 for the bird's body – two pieces meeting under main branch; main branch; bird's feet; dark glasses.

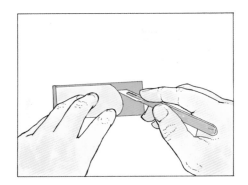

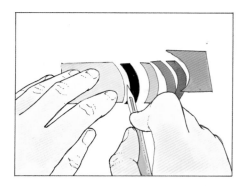

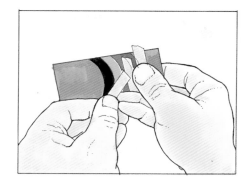

14 Make a template from $\frac{1}{16}$ in birch plywood or similar to mirror the shape where the beak joins the bird's head. Leaving enough for the back end of the beak, cut the shape of the template out of a piece of orange veneer.

15 Using the template, cut a series of narrow segments out of a selection of colored veneers. Finally, cut another piece of orange for the other end of the beak.

16 Glue these pieces together by rubbing a little glue on the edges and taping them together. When dry, remove the tape. Cut out the window for the beak and tape the prepared piece behind the window. Cut out and glue in place as before.

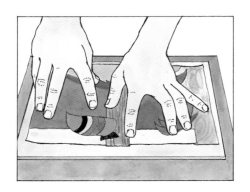

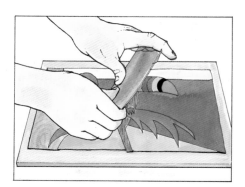

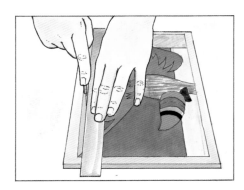

17 Remove all the tape and veneer the completed picture to a slightly oversize board. Remember to veneer the "right" side uppermost.

18 When it is dry, use a cabinet scraper to scrape the surface absolutely flat, noting the grain, direction of the pieces. You can scrape across the grain but do not work absolutely square as this can pull up the fibers and leave a rough surface. Do not sand to avoid colored dust in the grain.

19 Trim the edges square and form a border as required. Now mount as a picture or use the design as the lid for a box. Some very delicate designs can be made with this technique, and great levels of skill can be reached.

TUNBRIDGE-WARE

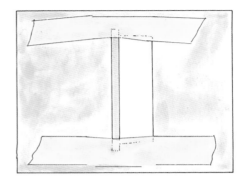

1 Tape a piece of waxed paper, $1 \times 3\frac{1}{4}$in, to a setting-up board and tape a piece of $\frac{1}{8}$in square boxwood or similar down the left side as shown.

This is a seemingly complex way of decorating boxes and other small items, but it is actually very straightforward. Traditionally, the whole piece to be decorated is covered in a series of identical, or similar, mosaic-like panels cut from the end of a made-up "log."

This log is formed from $\frac{1}{32}$in or $\frac{1}{16}$in square lines, glued together to produce something like a stick of rock with an identical design running the whole length. Different colored woods are used to produce the patterns; and ebony, boxwood, walnut, pear, and rosewood are all commonly used. Here, boxwood, padauk, and dyed veneer lines have been chosen. The black and red squares used are formed by taking $\frac{1}{16}$in slices off the edge of a laminated sheet of red and black veneers.

The basic method of producing a "log" is described here, but you will see that by making a log that is more and more complex. If you use a combination of different logs, extremely intricate and impressive designs can be gradually built up.

TOOLKIT AND MATERIALS

For basic kit, see pages 8-13	Setting-up board
Square boxwood or similar to provide a firm edge (see step 1)	Masking tape
	White glue (diluted)
Waxed paper	Veneers of your choice

Plan to show the arrangement of squares for the tunbridgeware log demonstrated here. Note that the outer boxwood squares go around three sides only.

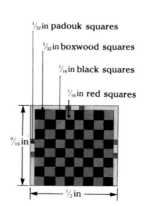

$\frac{1}{32}$in padouk squares

$\frac{1}{32}$in boxwood squares

$\frac{1}{16}$in black squares

$\frac{1}{16}$in red squares

$\frac{9}{16}$in

$\frac{1}{2}$in

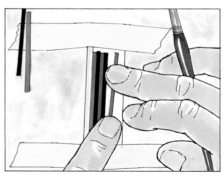

2 Cut 40 $\frac{1}{16}$in square strips, 20 each of black and red, $2\frac{3}{4}$in long from triple veneer "sandwiches." Put a red piece against the left-hand stop and brush 10 percent diluted white glue along its right-hand edge. Repeat for 10 pieces, alternately black and red.

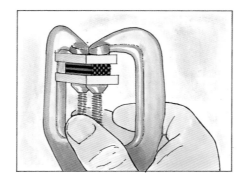

3 Place a piece of the boxwood square down the right-hand edge and tape it firmly in place. Repeat these steps until you have four identical pieces. Repeat to produce the two pieces of boxwood and padauk the same length and cut all pieces in two.

4 Glue and clamp four of the red/black pieces together, making sure that they are perfectly lined up at both ends. Protect the surfaces with scrap wood and repeat for the other four pieces. When both are dry, glue and clamp them together to produce one block.

5 When this block is dry, plane the four edges flush and square. Do this as little as possible; otherwise, you will be visibly reducing the dimensions of the outer layers of squares and spoiling the geometric effect.

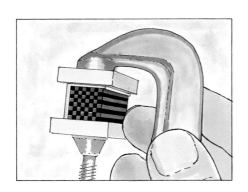

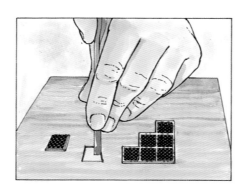

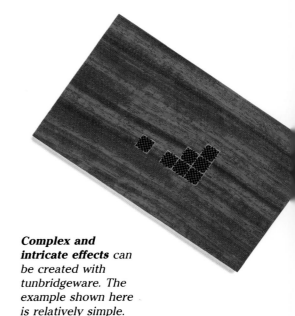

6 Now, one at a time, glue in place three of the four prepared boxwood and padauk pieces; they should be a little over-wide. Glue the first one in place with $\frac{1}{32}$ in of boxwood overhanging one long edge. The second piece should butt against this and so on.

7 When dry, trim the edges flush and cut $\frac{1}{16}$ in slivers off the end of the completed "log." Here some pieces have been combined and inlaid to form a geometric design.

Complex and intricate effects can be created with tunbridgeware. The example shown here is relatively simple.

Basic Finishing Methods

Wood comes to life when it is finished properly, and knowing how to apply a fine finish is one mark of a crafter. When to french polish, when to wax, and when to oil depends on the wood, the project, and the maker; and choosing between a high gloss and a soft luster can be a complex issue.

FRENCH POLISHING

French polish is the application of shellac dissolved in alcohol, which is gradually built up to a glorious, deep shine using a "rubber," or "pad". This is a small piece of cotton or batting folded into a piece of plain white cotton cloth and filled with polish.

Although it is a specific form of polish in its own right, French polish has become a generic term to describe many different polishes applied in the same way. Garnet polish is the darkest, and it is usually only appropriate for traditional or restoration work. Button is a more golden color, and French is a lighter version of this. Transparent polish is the most appropriate for light colored woods and dyed veneers. Beware, however, because transparent polish has a shelf life of only around 4 to 6 months.

It is usually necessary to fill the grain with a filler before you begin in order to avoid a lot of extra, time-consuming work filling with polish later on. There are many ways of filling grain – too many to mention here – but most modern fillers can be used (check the color first), and many are dry in 15 minutes.

The application of the polish is time-consuming. You must work slowly, using only a little polish at a time, and remember to use a small pad, no more than 1in long. For boxes, scale down your movements from what would be appropriate for, say, a table top.

Long, smooth, complete passes, oval shapes, circles, and figures-of-eight are all useful movements in French polishing. The order in which you use them is really up to you – you will be able to judge what is necessary by the way the polish is building up. You must maintain an even pressure – especially when doing circles – and the pad must keep moving.

Use only as much oil as is necessary to keep the pad working. Too much oil will give the piece a rather waxy, greasy finish, and curing it will require much hard work with alcohol and a nearly dry pad at the final stages when the work is being burnished.

The piece needs to be firmly held while you are working. If it is appropriate, you could drill a hole through the bottom and mount the whole box by screwing it into a piece of wood held in a vice – thus making it easy to change the angle of the box. If this is not possible, however, a piece of wood can be held in the vice to angle the box up toward you, held firm by hand pressure on the lid, which is worked last.

TOOLKIT AND MATERIALS

For basic kit, see pages 8-13	Cotton cloth
240/320/420-grit no-load sandpaper	Grain filler
1200-grit wet and dry sandpaper	Shellac sticks
0000 steel wool	Polish – French, button, or transparent
1in varnish or paintbrush	Mineral oil or linseed oil
Cotton batting	Denatured alcohol

French polishing, the king of finishes, brings perfection to a burl.

SURFACE PREPARATION

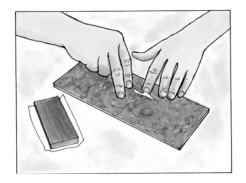

1 Sand the surface with 180-grit and then 240-grit garnet paper on a cork or cork-faced sanding block (see page 120, step 1). To remove dust, brush with a 2in wide varnish/paintbrush that is kept specially for this purpose.

2 If the piece was veneered, use the point of a craft knife to pick out any bits of glue or paper that have come through tiny knotholes or similar flaws during the veneering process.

3 Give the whole piece a coat of thinned sanding sealer, making sure that the surface is covered completely. When thoroughly dry, sand down using 240-grit no-load sandpaper.

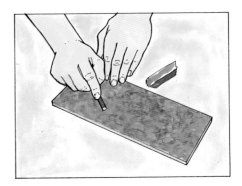

4 Fill any small holes using colored shellac sticks. Heat the end of a small screwdriver, melt a little of the shellac onto the end, and push it into the hole. The shellac will harden in seconds. Scrape off flush and sand.

5 Any open grain is best filled at this stage to save time filling in the grain with polish. Here, a water-based filler has been worked to a paste with a little water on a plate. A water dye can be added, or different colored fillers can be mixed.

6 When you have checked the color and you have a creamy, even consistency, rub the filler over the surface in all directions using a piece of cotton cloth. Finish by rubbing across the grain to push as much filler as possible into the grain and remove any excess.

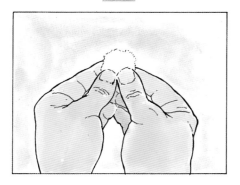

7 When dry, sand gently with 320-grit no-load sandpaper. Work until the figure of the wood reappears. When finishing burled walnut or a similar highly figured wood, you may need to use two or more different colored filling pastes for the different areas.

8 Inspect the surface and fill in any slight pits that the paste hasn't quite filled. When dry, sand lightly, dust thoroughly, and brush on a coat of full-strength sanding sealer. Sand lightly with 240-grit no-load sandpaper and, again, dust thoroughly.

9 To make a pad, take a small piece of cotton or batting about 2in square and form it into a ball by folding in the four corners underneath itself.

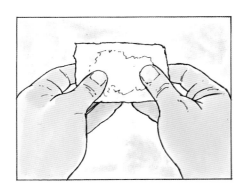

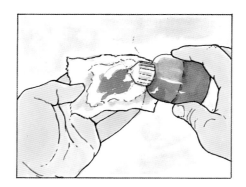

10 Place this "ball" with the corners facing upward on a piece of polishing rag 2×3in and allow the corners to spring open a little.

11 Fill the batting liberally with polish. It is best to keep your polish in a plastic container with a small "nozzle." A dishwashing detergent bottle is ideal for larger jobs, but is not really appropriate for the small amounts used for boxes.

12 Now wrap the rag around the filled batting to produce a smooth, flat, crease-free surface that should be about 1in across. Press this onto a piece of clean paper to squeeze out excess polish. This is your pad.

APPLYING THE POLISH

13 Work the pad along the length of the piece to be polished in slow, firm movements until you have covered the whole surface. The more you press, the more polish you will deposit on the surface. With practice you will be able to gauge pressure accurately.

14 When you have worked over the whole surface, refill the pad and apply one or two drops of mineral oil. This will allow the pad to move freely over the surface of the work.

15 The pad must always be kept moving when it is in contact with the work; otherwise, it will stick and spoil the developing shine. Continue to work over the whole surface, using complete strokes across the grain.

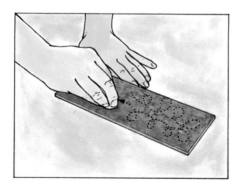

16 Then start to use circular motions, adding a drop more oil if necessary. When you are polishing a box or any other small item, it is important not to spend too much time working on any one face. Alternate the faces regularly to prevent them from becoming sticky.

17 Now revert to complete passes the full length of the piece. Edges and corners tend to be neglected, so remember – work well into the corners and edges, and the center will look after itself.

18 Stop when a good body of polish has built up. Put a little denatured alcohol on the pad and put it in a plastic bag inside a small, airtight container to keep the pad moist for the next session.

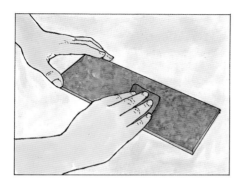

19 Leave the polished piece to harden overnight, then sand the surface lightly with 320-grit no-load sandpaper. There is not a sandpaper made that will not clog with French polish, particularly when it is freshly applied. Discard the pieces after only a little use.

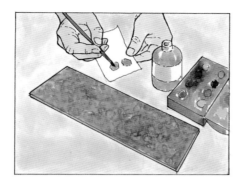

20 Check if the colors of the grain fillers used are blending as they should. Correct discrepancies using an artist's brush dipped in polish, then into alcohol dye powder. The color can be blended on the back of a piece of used sandpaper.

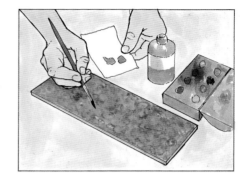

21 Carefully brush a small amount of the blended color onto the required place and check the result. With a little practice, almost any blemish can be camouflaged. It is often useful to go back to your basic polish and use this to blend your color.

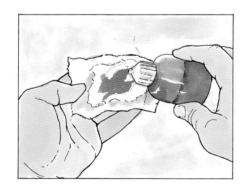

22 These color corrections can be gently sanded before you proceed, but it is generally best to build up a bit more polish first. Refill the pad and continue as before, alternating cross grain, circular and along-the-grain strokes. Dry for a further 24 hours.

23 Fill the pad with less polish than before. Add a few drops of denatured alcohol to the face of the pad and one drop of oil. Start working with the grain, then across, then in circles and finally with the grain again.

24 Continue to work the surface, using less and less polish and a little more denatured alcohol; finally use only one or two drops of alcohol and rub with increasing pressure until completely dry. Set aside for a few days. Sand gently and repeat the final burnishing stage.

SEALING AND WAXING

On close-grained woods, such as maple or good-quality mahogany, sealing and waxing yields a finish with a wonderful sheen that is beautifully smooth to the touch. On open-grained woods it produces a finish similar to oiling, but far more quickly. The thinned shellac sanding sealer takes only about an hour to dry. It can then be sanded and waxed immediately and then needs only to be buffed with a soft cloth after a few minutes.

A grain filler is usually not necessary or appropriate, but if you feel you need to do this or fill larger holes and flaws, see page 116. Shellac sanding sealer has a high solid content, which fills grain very effectively. It is available in several colors, but the palest is the most generally useful. When dry, it sands easily, producing an ultrafine white powder.

| 1 | Smooth wood thoroughly using sandpaper wrapped around a sanding block. Garnet paper is best for sanding bare, unfinished wood. First use 180-grit, which removes all unevenness, and then smooth it further with 240-grit, sanding along the grain. |

APPLYING SEALER

| 2 | Remove all dust by brushing the work with a 2in-wide varnish/paintbrush, that is kept especially for this purpose. Apply shellac sanding sealer, thinned 3 to 1 with denatured alcohol. Brush this first across, and then along, the grain. |

TOOLKIT AND MATERIALS

For basic kit, see pages 8-13

1in varnish/paintbrush

1200-grit wet and dry paper

0000 steel wool

Shellac sanding sealer, thinned by $\frac{1}{3}$ denatured alcohol

Fine paste wax, color as required

Sealing and waxing *is the traditional way of protecting and enhancing wood.*

3 The sealer will be dry to the touch after about 20 minutes. Allow it to dry for at least three hours to give it time to harden properly. Now sand gently using 320-grit no-load sandpaper. If the sealer is completely dry, this will produce a fine white powder.

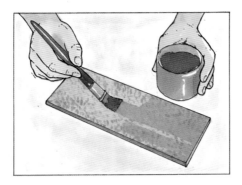

4 Remove the dust as before with a clean dry brush and apply another coat of thinned sanding sealer, working only along the grain this time. Allow to harden as before.

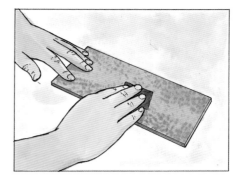

5 Now sand very gently, with the grain, using 1200-grit wet and dry sandpaper. Don't use the block, just light finger pressure. Work in full passes to avoid causing scratch marks made when the direction of the sandpaper is changed.

APPLYING WAX

6 Apply the wax to the surface with 0000 steel wool. Work in complete passes along the grain. Use only a little wax. Now apply a little more with a soft cloth. Work it in small circular movements.

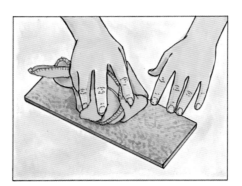

7 Allow to dry for a few minutes and then buff with a clean, soft cloth. Repeat two or three times to bring out a fine, silky sheen. Don't allow the wax to harden for too long, as you will have to work harder to remove any excess.

8 For a more flat finish, apply the wax with the steel wool, moving it in a circular motion over the surface, starting quite firmly and gradually becoming gentler. Allow the wax to harden for a few minutes and buff as before.

OIL FINISH

Oiling is a wonderful finish for pieces made from solid, open-grained woods such as oak or ash, or for closer grained woods for which a bright finish is not required. The oil should be applied when the wood has been sanded smooth and, normally, no grain filling is employed.

Linseed oil is the original English oak finish. Of the two forms readily available, raw linseed oil is marginally harder-wearing, but it takes two to three days for an application to harden. Applications of boiled linseed oil take around 24 hours to harden.

Specially prepared oils, such as Danish and teak oils, dry harder and faster than linseed oil and provide slightly more protection. Three or four applications are normally necessary, depending on the porosity of the wood, which should be lightly sanded between each application.

| 1 | It is important to have a smooth, well-sanded and dust-free surface to start with. Sand the surface then thoroughly remove all trace of dust (for more details, see page 120, steps 1-2). You are then ready to go ahead. |

TOOLKIT AND MATERIALS

For basic kit, see pages 8-13

———

Soft cotton cloth

———

0000 steel wool

———

400-grit no-load sandpaper (for Danish and teak oils)

Raw linseed oil (drying time 3 days); boiled linseed oil (drying time 24 hours); teak oil (drying time 12 hours); Danish oil (drying time 12 hours)

APPLYING OIL

| 2 | Cut a 4in square piece of soft cloth, such as cheesecloth. This is available by the yard, and this is the cheapest way to buy it. |

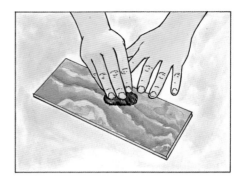

3 Form this piece into a pad and hold with a crease-free, single surface exposed. Fill this liberally with oil. A half-and-half mixture of boiled linseed oil and mineral spirits is being used here; the latter aids absorption in the early stages.

4 Rub the oil evenly and firmly over the surface, working across the grain, in circles, and finally with the grain to maintain an even and complete covering. Set aside for 24 hours to dry. Repeat with one more thinned coat and set aside to harden for a further 24 hours.

5 Apply two more coats of the full-strength, undiluted oil, allowing time to dry between each coat as before. When the final coat is dry, rub over the whole surface with 0000 grade steel wool, starting with circular movements and finishing with full, even passes with the grain.

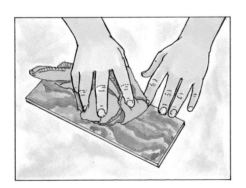

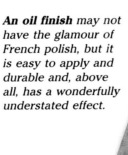

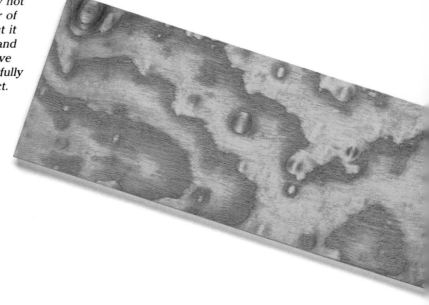

6 Buff with a soft cloth to produce an even, rich, and natural-looking flat finish. If a slightly less matte look is what you have in mind, do not rub with the steel wool, but merely buff with a clean, soft cloth to produce a glowing, silky-smooth sheen.

An oil finish may not have the glamour of French polish, but it is easy to apply and durable and, above all, has a wonderfully understated effect.

Boxmaker's Gallery

The art and craft of box-making exists all over the world. From producing the purely practical to constructing the charmingly bizarre, box-making is a common and fulfilling occupation. A look at the richness and variety of the work of others will stir your imagination and lead you to new and fascinating projects.

TURNED BOX

JOHN AMBROSE

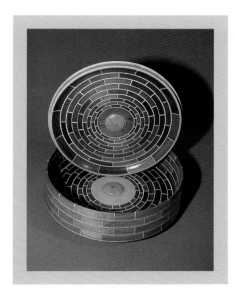

Turning is a technique that is traditionally used to produce small- and medium-sized containers, with or without lids. The blank from which this beautifully made "brickwork" lidded box was turned was formed by using teak "bricks" with sycamore joints. In work of this kind, it is essential that the joints of the blank fit perfectly; otherwise, the piece will fall apart when it is turned.

JEWELRY BOX

JOHN BURKE

Plywood is normally used as a base on which veneer is laid. Here, however, good-quality birch plywood has been laminated to several thicknesses and cut on a bandsaw to produce the unusual lid. The sides are mahogany, and the finials on the end of the hinge pin are ebony.

PENCIL BOX

ANDREW CRAWFORD

The tambour lid of this two-tier pencil box is made from thin strips of beautifully figured snakewood, which have been glued to a piece of thread. The lid runs in a groove, which curves down and under the top compartment of the box. The framework and drawer are made of American black walnut, and the mitered corners have been strengthened with "fake" dovetails.

SHAKER BOXES

A. B. WOODWORKING

Shaker furniture is characterized by its simplicity, and every design is informed by the belief that each item should serve as perfectly as possible its appointed purpose. These boxes were made in the traditional Shaker way by soaking the wood in hot water and bending it around a mold. The red box is made from Finnish birch plywood; the blue box is American cherry. Both boxes have been colored with traditional American buttermilk paint.

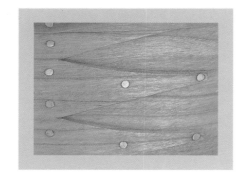

JEWELRY BOX

KENNETH BOWERS

Below: The subtly curved sides of this simple rectangular box soften the rather austere outlines and help to make the shape more interesting. The English walnut framework has dovetailed corners, and the inlay is of yew, laburnum, harewood (stained sycamore), ebony, and holly.

RUSSIAN BOX

MAKER UNKNOWN

Right: The intricate geometric patterns, although apparently achieved by parquetry, were in fact created by gluing accurately cut pieces of straw onto the completed framework. Because no inlaying is involved, this is a relatively simple, although time-consuming and painstaking, way of producing a highly decorative result. Careful planning and laying out beforehand are, of course, essential.

JEWELRY BOX

ANDREW CRAWFORD

Below: The unusual shape of this jewelry box is emphasized by the geometric, parquetry-style decoration. The lid and front are bordered by a multicolored decorative line, made from dyed veneers. The lid opens to reveal a dark green silk- and velvet-lined interior with two ebony trays.

COLLECTOR'S BOX

MAX COOPER

Quality is evident in every line and detail of this beautifully designed and exquisitely executed oval collector's box. The veneered satinwood is decorated with neoclassical marquetry motifs and cross-banding in Rio rosewood and with boxwood and ebony lines. Hidden spring catches release the two doors, which open to reveal six bow-fronted, dovetailed drawers, made from ebony veneered in Rio rosewood. The turned knobs are boxwood. The contrast between the rich yellow satinwood and the dark brown and black rosewood further underlines the quality of the construction.

JEWELRY BOX

PETER STONHILL

Inlaid sycamore and walnut basket-weave panels have been used to decorate this traditionally styled, domed-top jewelry box. The ends of each piece of sycamore were dipped into hot sand and scorched to produce the shading effect. The panels themselves are bordered in purpleheart. The interior, which has two dovetailed trays, is lined with aromatic cedar of Lebanon.

MARQUETRY BOX

MAKER UNKNOWN

Some makers use boxes simply as a vehicle for showing off a particular technique. This Polish piece, for example, is really a beautifully cut marquetry panel with a box attached. The panel features many different woods. Notice how burls have been used to represent the different kinds of foliage, while ripple sycamore was used for the sky; and other, carefully selected, grains and colors have been used for additional details.

CLOCK AND CASE

ROBERT SAXBY

Below: This clock by Robert Saxby uses straight lines and the stark contrast between wenge and ash to produce a piece of deceptive simplicity. The proportions and the exact positions of the diagonal lines have been carefully thought out to give a feel of balance.

COLLECTOR'S BOX

IAN FORSBERG

Above: The design for this stunning and unusual piece was inspired by the form of the traditional Japanese family shrine. It is made in English brown oak and jacaranda, and the techniques used include curved lamination. The tambour doors have been pulled back to reveal the inner container.

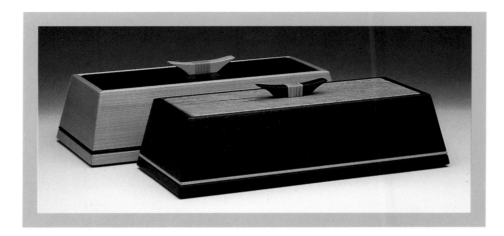

WENGE AND MAPLE BOXES

LARRY DERN

Both of these boxes are made from combinations of wenge and maple, woods that contrast well with each other. They are sleekly shaped and well proportioned, which are important considerations in the construction of all types of box. The sloped sides, which give the boxes something of the appearance of gold ingots, create an impression of mass and solidity, but the strong, geometric lines are softened by the elegantly shaped finials.

SCULPTED BOX

KEN ALTMAN

Below: Although it is small, this high-quality box has been exquisitely sculpted. It is made from beautifully figured Greek briar burl, which contrasts perfectly with the pure black of the ebony. The gold and micarta add the finishing luxurious touches.

WRITING BOX

PETER LLOYD

The slightly wayward quality of the solid burl oak from which it was made has been mirrored and subtly emphasized by the gentle contouring of the outside of this box. The construction features lapped (half-blind) dovetails and the wood hinges – also in burl oak – are glued and dowelled in place. Inside the box are two dovetailed sycamore trays and a drawer for paper, all of which are lined in leather.

JEWELRY BOX

PAULA E. COOPERRIDER

Solid Indian rosewood was selected for the framework of this jewelry box. The simple lines of the beautifully figured rosewood contrast wonderfully with the ornately carved and detailed laurel hinges and drawer pulls.

BURL ELM BOX

DAVID GREGSON

This box, with its strong, straight lines, has been designed to allow the beauty of the wood to speak for itself. The impact of the intricate figuring of the slabs of solid burl elm has not been diminished in any way by additional decoration, and the overall impression of mass is further reinforced by the square, solid ebony feet, handle, and studs.

BOAT BOX

JOHN ANDERSON

Below: If further proof were needed that a box does not need to be "box" shaped, this intriguing box has been carved in the shape of a boat from a piece of solid jelutong. The lid is hinged at the back, and acrylic paints were used for the cheerful decoration.

WALNUT BOX

ARTHUR "ESPENET" CARPENTER

Above: A flaw in the piece of walnut selected for the lid has been combined with a small cutaway in the front to create a humorous "face." Inlays of bone and ebony for the "eyes" and "nose" complete the effect, making what is basically a simple box into a unique and characterful piece.

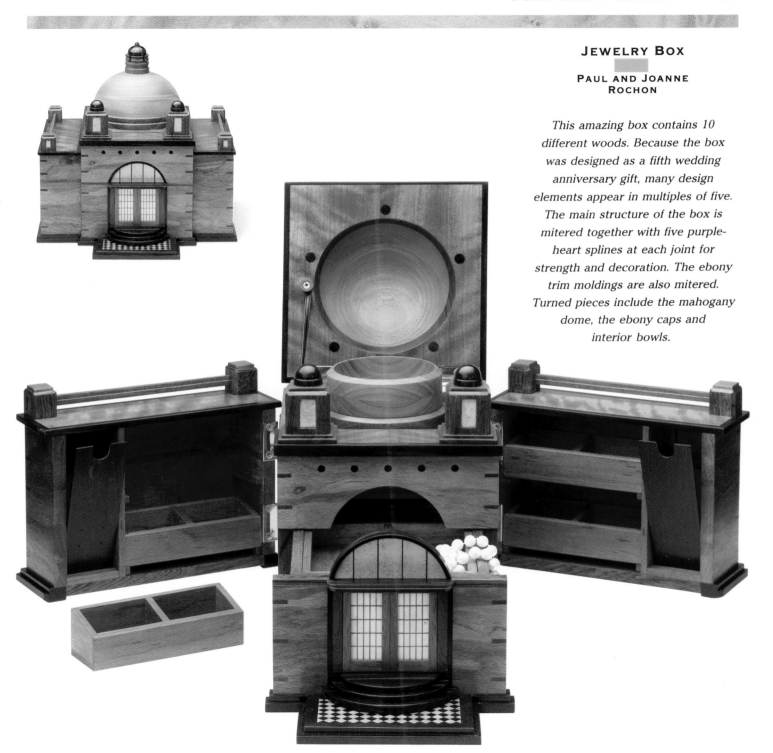

JEWELRY BOX

PAUL AND JOANNE ROCHON

This amazing box contains 10 different woods. Because the box was designed as a fifth wedding anniversary gift, many design elements appear in multiples of five. The main structure of the box is mitered together with five purple-heart splines at each joint for strength and decoration. The ebony trim moldings are also mitered. Turned pieces include the mahogany dome, the ebony caps and interior bowls.

TREASURE CHEST

ROBERT INGHAM

Although this chest appears to be veneered, it is, in fact, a frame-and-panel construction, consisting of as many as 80 small panels of burl elm held in frames of bog oak. The immaculately made lining and trays are ripple sycamore, and the brasswork fittings were designed and made as integral elements of the overall design.

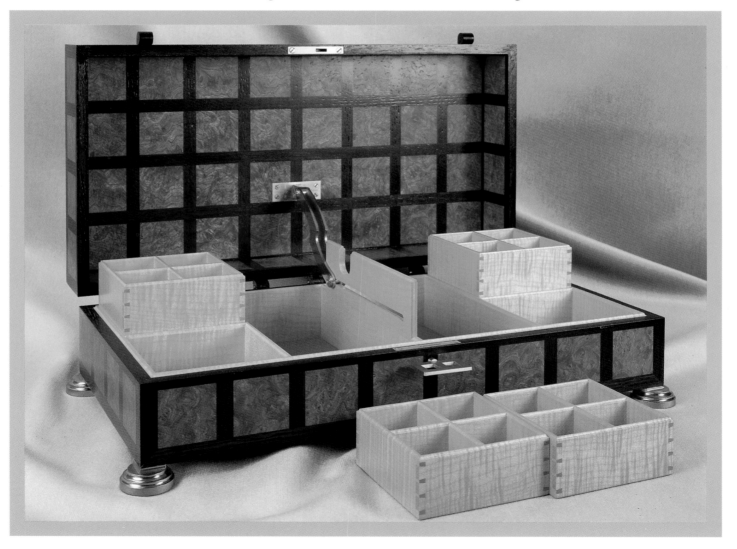

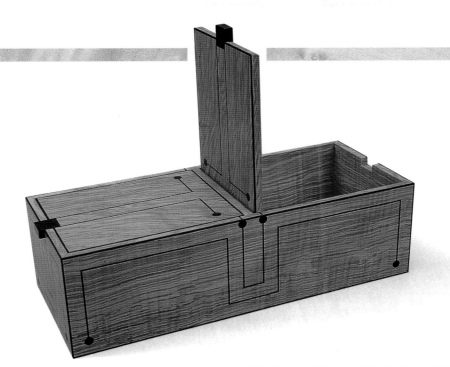

INDEX CARD BOX

ROBERT INGHAM

Left: Anyone who has a rather tired and scratched plastic index-card holder will marvel at this sleekly designed box. It is beautifully constructed from olive ash and has secret dovetails. The contrasting detail lines and inlays are bog oak, and the lids are hinged with bog oak pegs.

JEWELRY BOX

CHRISTOPHER VICKERS

Right: The basic structure of this simple, elegant box is oak, which has been veneered with burled yew. Holly was used for the detailing, and the velvet-lined trays are maple. All the joints are mitered and strengthened with veneer keys. The attention to detail lavished on the woodwork has been extended to the use of matching escutcheon and bun feet.

PERFUME CASKET

STEPHEN FIELD

This superbly made and complex piece is richly decorated with panels in amboyna, one of the most expensive woods available. These are bordered with ebony, and the exterior is further enhanced with Egyptian-style silver-gilt mountings, contrasting beautifully with both woods. Stringing lines are in boxwood and ebony.

The inset shows the lid open to reveal a lavishly fitted interior lined with peacock blue silk and containing eight St. Louis crystal perfume bottles. A secret drawer containing a manicure set is revealed by operating a finial inside the central compartment.

WATERCOLOR BOX

ANDREW CRAWFORD

This striking watercolor box made by the author is veneered with Canadian maple and decorated with dyed veneers. The comprehensively fitted interior contains all a watercolorist could possibly need; and on pulling a small, turned boxwood finial, a dovetailed drawer springs out, revealing a second palette.

The wavy inlaid lines are made by cutting strips from a layer of veneers made by laminating them in a curved former.

BRIDGE BOX

JIM BEATTIE

The simple lines of this padouk-veneered plywood bridge box provide the perfect background for the elegantly cut marquetry silhouettes that decorate its two sections.

The interior is designed to contain two decks of cards with pencils and score pads. The top of the lid is inlaid with the four suits, and the knob and pointer can be turned to indicate which suit is trump.

Glossary

Batting Absorbent cotton wool around which a piece of cotton fabric is wrapped to form the rubber used in *French polishing*.

Bead A simple, rounded, decorative molding.

Beading scraper A small, improvised scraper made from a hacksaw blade or similar and used to produce a bead molding.

Birch plywood The best quality plywood, which is available in thicknesses from $\frac{1}{16}$ in up.

Bottom cut A straight router bit with "bottom cut" will cut at the bottom, as well as at the sides, of a groove or *rabbet*.

Burl veneer The *veneer* taken from areas of the tree where abnormal growth or the root has caused a highly decorative grain pattern.

Button polish A dark gold-colored *French polish*.

C-clamps Essential workshop equipment in a variety of sizes and shapes, all basically C-shaped, and used to hold two pieces of wood together, often while adhesive dries.

Carpenter's mallet A wooden mallet that does not damage the handles of chisels.

Caul A piece of wood, often curved upward at each end, used in veneering to transfer pressure from a pair of clamps to the center of a wide board. Also used to describe a complete, shaped piece for veneering a shaped panel.

Chamfer A corner that is beveled to an angle of 45 degrees.

Cheese cloth A finely woven, multi-purpose cloth used for finishing; available from hardware stores.

Core The central, decorative portion of a decorative line or banding.

Countersink bit The bit for an electric drill that is used to create the seating for the head of a countersunk screw.

Cross-banding Decorative line consisting of an outer line or lines and an inner core of a figured wood with the grain running at right angles.

Curved scraper A curved cabinet scraper used to smooth concave shapes. Also known as a gooseneck scraper.

Dado A groove or channel cut across the grain.

Danish oil A good oil for wood finishing, faster drying than *linseed oil*.

Dovetail An efficient and decorative, albeit painstaking, joint of interlocking, fan-shaped elements, used to hold two pieces of wood at a right angle.

End-grain The end of a piece of wood exposed by a cut across the grain.

Escutcheon A decorative plate into which a keyhole is cut, either applied externally or inlaid.

Fence A piece of timber or metal used to guide work being machined in a straight line and at a fixed distance from the blade/cutter. Also the adjustable part of a woodworking machine that achieves the same end when used freehand.

Framework The basic shell of a box or item of furniture.

French polish The generic name given to a mixture of *shellac* and mineral spirits, traditionally used as a finish for fine furniture.

Garnet paper A good-quality, long-lasting sandpaper for use on plain, unfinished wood.

Garnet polish A dark brown *French polish*.

Grain filler A substance, available in many forms and colors, used to fill in the grain or flaws in wood before it is finished.

Guide pin An integral guide on a router bit that guarantees that the depth of a cut is consistent. It obviates the need for a *fence*.

Heartwood The hard, non-living wood at the core of a tree trunk, usually darker in color than *sapwood*.

Hollow plane A wooden plane with a convex sole used to form concave sections.

Hook The tiny amount of metal turned over when a cabinet scraper is sharpened (burnished).

Jig An improvised aid made to facilitate a particular, often repetitive, task.

Knuckle The rounded, interlocking parts of a hinge.

Linseed oil The traditional finish for English oak; it may be used raw or boiled.

Lip and spur The best arrangement of a high-speed drill bit for cutting clean, accurately positioned holes in wood.

Lipping A thin sliver of contrasting or decorative wood used to face the top or front edge of a different wood.

Log A piece made from fine, hardwood strips, glued together and used to make Tunbridgeware.

Marquetry The art of combining veneers of different colors and figurings to produce pictures.

MDF (Medium Density Fiberboard) A stable, good-quality, man-made board, often veneered. Also called particle board.

Miter A simple joint in which both pieces are cut at equal angles to bisect a joint. Most often, the pieces are cut to angles of 45 degrees to create a joint of 90 degrees, although the angles can be more or less than 45 degrees. A miter joint may be strengthened by *splines*.

Miter trimmer Two lever-operated, vertically mounted blades used to trim rough-sawn miter joints. The blades are set at angles of 45 degrees to an adjustable *fence*.

Moldings Strips of wood, shaped by a molding plane or router and used to decorate wooden objects.

Needle files Small files, available in a variety of profiles, used for fine shaping.

No-load sandpaper Abrasive paper for sanding French polish, varnish, etc., which is impregnated with a fine lubricant to resist clogging and make the paper last longer.

Ovolo A convex *molding* profile that is a quarter of a circle in cross-section.

Parquetry The art of combining identical shapes of veneer or solid wood to create geometric patterns.

Pass The single movement of a plane along a piece of wood or the movement of a piece of wood through a machine.

Piano hinge Continuous hinge available in lengths, both drilled with holes and undrilled.

Plank A piece formed from laminated *veneers* from which inlay lines and bandings are cut.

Purfling The fine decorative edging around the bodies of some stringed instruments.

Purfling cutter The adjustable tool used to remove a fine rabbet from around the edges of violins, guitars, etc., in order to add *purfling*. Also useful in fine cabinetwork.

P.V.A. (Poly-vinyl Acetate) A general-purpose, water-based white or yellow wood adhesive. Widely used for craft and hobby work.

Quadrant hinge An attractive hinge that incorporates an integral stay to stop the lid at an opening of 90 degrees.

Quarter-sawn Stable wood that has been cut radially – i.e., along the radius of the trunk.

Radius bit A router bit designed to produce a quarter- or half-round concave section.

Rabbet A square recess along the edge of a piece of wood. Also known as a rebate.

Right-angle guide A *jig* made to hold a piece of wood at right angles to a fence to facilitate accurate machining of the end grain.

Rounding-over bit A bit cutter designed to produce a quarter-round convex section along the edge of a piece of wood.

Router table A purpose-built or improvised platform under which a router is mounted so that it protrudes through a hole in the table's surface.

Rubber A pad, made from cotton batting and covered with cotton sheeting, used to apply *French polish*.

Sanding drum A drill-mounted drum, the outer face of which is covered with sandpaper, that is most useful when the drill is used in a drill stand.

Sanding sealer A useful *shellac*- or cellulose-based, multi-purpose sealer with a high content of solids so that it fills grain well. Available in a variety of colors, although transparent is most useful.

Sandwich Multilayer piece glued together from several sheets of veneer.

Sapwood The living wood from the outer part of a tree trunk, which is often lighter in color than the *heartwood*.

Sash-clamp A clamp with a long reach, originally used for gluing the frames of sash windows. Also known as a bar-cramp.

Scraper burnisher A piece of hardened steel, usually round in section and mounted in a handle, designed to form the *hook* along the edges of a *cabinet scraper*.

Set The slight offset of alternate teeth on the blade of a saw that permits the clearance of sawdust and prevents the blade from binding.

Shellac The resin secreted by the lac beetle, which is dissolved in mineral spirits to form the basis of *French polish*.

Sliding bevel A tool with a handle and a sliding steel portion, which can be set to any angle, used for laying out dovetails, etc.

Slot bit A router bit formed from a cutting disk mounted on an arbor and designed to cut slots at 90 degrees to the axis of the router.

Smoothing plane A useful, multi-purpose plane for box-making that is capable of fine adjustment.

Sole The base of a plane.

Spline A thin sliver of wood glued in to a slot sawn horizontally across a *miter* to strengthen the joint.

Spline jig A *jig* designed to allow the slots for splines to be cut on a router.

Step and stop An improvised set-up that allows the plane to be used on its side to plane the edge of a piece of wood.

Straight bit A router bit used to make square and rectangular sections, grooves, rabbets, etc.

Tangentially sawn Wood that has been cut at a tangent to the trunk of a tree. Planks sawn in this way are less stable than quarter-sawn planks.

Teak oil A good, fast-drying oil finish.

Template A piece of thin, rigid material that has been accurately cut to facilitate the repeated precise marking of a shape. Also known as a templet.

Tongue The portion of wood left when a *rabbet* has been cut along the end grain of a piece of wood.

Transparent polish An almost transparent kind of *French polish*, suitable for enhancing the figure of light-colored woods. It has a shelf-life of only 4-6 months.

Tunbridgeware A traditional British form of decoration formed from complex patterns made from pieces sliced from a *log* prepared from thin strips of hardwood.

Tungsten carbide bits The best quality and longest lasting, although most expensive, router bits.

Veneer Extremely thin sheets of wood, knife-cut or sawn from *logs* and traditionally used when solid wood would be too expensive, unstable, or mechanically weak.

Veneercraft A simple, easy, and quick form of decoration in which veneered shapes are glued to a background to produce a motif or picture, often in several layers. The pieces are not inlaid flush as in *marquetry*.

Veneering press A press available in many formats and sizes used for veneering panels. A small steel platform exerts pressure over the whole area by means of a single, sturdy, centrally mounted fly screw.

Wet and dry paper Sandpaper than can be used wet to cut back synthetic finishes and paints. Available in very fine grits that, when used dry, are excellent for cutting back *French polish*, etc.

Window A shaped portion cut out of the prepared background for a *marquetry* picture through which the piece to fit it is cut.

INDEX

CREDITS

Quarto would like to thank the following for permission to reproduce copyright material. While every effort has been made to trace and acknowledge all copyright holders, we would like to apologize if any omissions have been made.

Key: T=top; B=bottom; L=left; R=right; M=middle; TR=top right; TL=top left; BR=bottom right

Page 16 T Andrew Crawford; **page 16** B David Gregson; **page 17** John Anderson; **page 18** John S. Ambrose; **page 125** L John S. Ambrose; **page 125** M John Burke; **page 125** TR Andrew Crawford; **page 126** T&M Anthony's Boxes/A.B Woodworking, Shropshire; **page 126** B Kenneth E. Bowers; **page 127** T Quarto Publishing Plc; **page 127** B Andrew Crawford; **page 128** Max Cooper; **page 129** T Peter Stonhill; **page 129** B Quarto Publishing Plc; **page 130** TL Ian Forsberg; **page 130** BR J. Robert Saxby; **page 131** TL Larry Dern/The Rosen Group; **page 131** BR Ken Altman; **page 132** T&B Peter Lloyd; **page 133** T Paula E. Cooperrider.